HEALTHY OILS

Including the Health Benefits of Omega-3

HEALTHY OILS

Including the Health Benefits of Omega-3

Lee Faber

Abbeydale Press

ISBN 978-1-86147-236-6

1 3 5 7 9 10 8 6 4 2

Published by Abbeydale Press
an imprint of Bookmart Ltd
Registered number 2372865
Trading as Bookmart Ltd
Blaby Road, Wigston, Leicester
LE18 4SE, England

Produced for Bookmart Limited
Illustrations by Tegan Sharrard
Cover design by Omnipress Ltd

Printed in Dubai

ABOUT THE AUTHOR

Lee Faber is a native American who became a British
citizen, having been in the UK since 1981. She has
lived and worked in New York, Florida, London and
now resides in Wiltshire.

During her career she has been involved in book
editing and writing with an emphasis on health, food
and cookery. She has specialised in Americanising/
Anglicising books on a variety of subjects for both
US and UK publishers.

She is an accomplished cook and has created many
recipes.

CONTENTS

Introduction

Fat doesn't always make you fat!

At one point in history not so very long ago, in Britain we cooked exclusively with butter and margarine, lard, suet and solid fat.

Butter was very popular because it imparted a rich flavour to both cooked and baked foods. Lard was extremely practical as an all-purpose cooking fat and for use in baking as it produced the most tender and flaky pastry crusts. Suet was used for the creation of dumplings and for several traditional English steamed puddings, such as steak and kidney pudding. Margarine was used as a cheaper alternative to butter.

They are all saturated fats.

Saturated fats are those fats that are solid at room temperature. They are nearly always from animal sources. Coconut oil and palm oil are vegetable sources of saturated fats. Saturated fat raises the level of cholesterol in the blood. Elevated cholesterol levels are responsible for a number of modern ailments. So we have been warned to decrease the amount of saturated fats in our diet and replace them with unsaturated fats which are supposed to be healthier.

You've all seen the television adverts for a certain brand of olive oil which depicts a very aged population doing all sorts of things that only young people usually do. Until quite recently, we believed that olive oil was the 'healthy' oil and we ought to be doing more with it than just putting it in salad dressing.

But olive is not the only healthy oil.

There are numerous oils and fats obtained from plant and animal sources that are used for hundreds of culinary, pharmaceutical and cosmetic products. Some of the oils and fats are produced by refining or rendering processes that usually involve heat and some are simply obtained through cold-pressing.* Oils that are obtained through cold extraction, such as olive oil and rapeseed oil, are usually more expensive than refined oils and fats obtained through high heat extraction methods, but they retain all their flavour, aroma and nutritional value.

All oils and fats are 100% fat, but the components that make up the fat structure of a particular oil are important in determining whether or not the oil or fat is considered healthy. While some oils such as olive and rapeseed are considered very healthy, all oils are high in calories (about 120 calories per tablespoon) so they should be consumed in moderation.

However, it is a myth to believe that the consumption of fat makes you fat. Fats provide a concentrated source of energy. A certain amount of fat is necessary in every healthy person's diet.

Many of the oils we talk about in this book have been around for thousands of years and we are rediscovering their healthy aspects that our ancestors knew about centuries ago.

*Cold-pressing refers to oils obtained through pressing and grinding fruit or seeds using heavy granite millstones or modern stainless steel presses. Although pressing and grinding produces heat through friction, in order to label an oil cold-pressed, the temperature of the oil must not rise above 49°C/120°F. Expeller-pressing is similar to cold-pressing, except that extreme pressure is used, resulting in much higher temperatures.

Culinary Oils and their Characteristics

FRUIT OILS

APRICOT KERNEL OIL

Apricot kernel oil is obtained from the dried kernels of the apricot tree. The oil is usually cold- or expeller-pressed. Some brands may use additional refining procedures, which do not allow the oil to be labelled cold-pressed or unrefined. It is high in monounsaturated fat and contains no trans-fatty acids, so it is a very healthy oil. It is suitable for high heat cooking methods, such as sautéing and pan-frying, and the mild flavour makes it a good choice for salad dressings. It is also popular as a massage oil and carrier for aromatherapy oils. Apricot kernel oil is most often available in gourmet and health food shops.

AVOCADO OIL

Avocado oil has a light, but unique flavour that makes it an excellent choice for salad dressings, for roasting vegetables or as a seasoning. It is usually produced from avocados that are damaged or not aesthetically pleasing. Refined avocado oil has the highest smoke point* of any plant oil, so it is useful for high heat cooking. Avocado oil is a good source of monounsaturated fat and vitamin E, which makes it nutritionally beneficial. Avocado oil can be found in some supermarkets and speciality shops.

COCONUT OIL

Coconut oil is extracted from the dried meat of the coconut and is very popular in India and Southeast Asia. It solidifies at room temperature and has a buttery texture. Coconut oil contains a high level of saturated fat (92%). It is generally agreed among nutritionists and health professionals that foods with high levels of saturated fat should be avoided, but this may not be true with coconut oil. There are several studies that have indicated that the saturated fat in coconut oil metabolises in the body similar to an unsaturated fat and

---

*The *smoke point* refers to the temperature at which a cooking fat or oil begins to break down. The substance smokes or burns, and gives food an unpleasant taste. Beyond the smoke point is the flash point, the point at which combustion occurs.

as a result, LDL (low-density lipoprotein — bad cholesterol) will not increase. However, in promoting healthy food choices the British Heart Foundation and others are sceptical concerning the health benefits of coconut oil. It is widely used in commercial baked goods, confectionery, non-dairy whipped topping and coffee creamers and as a cooking fat.

GRAPE SEED OIL
Grape seed oil is a by-product of the winemaking industry. The majority of oil extracted from grape seeds is produced in France, Switzerland and Italy, but there are also a few producers in the United States. The subtle flavour of grape seed oil is well suited for many types of salads because the oil will not overpower the other ingredients. It may also be combined with stronger-flavoured, more expensive oils, which makes them more economical to use. Refined grape seed oil has a high smoke point so it is an excellent choice as a cooking oil, especially when sautéing or frying.

OLIVE OIL

Olive oil is obtained from the olive tree *Olea europaea*, a traditional crop of the Mediterranean area. It is a healthy oil because of its high content of monounsaturated fat. Olive oil has been one of the staples of the Mediterranean diet for thousands of years and its popularity has grown rapidly in other parts of the world. It is one of the most versatile oils for cooking and it enhances the taste of many foods. It is an excellent alternative to butter or margarine as a spread, or for use in food preparation.

There are three basic types of olive oil available: extra virgin, virgin and just plain olive oil. To be classified as extra virgin, the acidity level of the oil can be no greater than 1%. It is best to use extra virgin for dishes in which the olive oil will not be heated, such as in salads or as a spread or dip.

Virgin olive oil has a maximum acidity of 2% and can be used just like the higher grade. It is much more reasonably priced and is versatile in that it can be used generously in cooking and yet it has enough flavour to be used in salads or as a condiment.

Products labelled 'olive oil' or 'pure olive oil' usually have a ratio of 85% refined oil to 15% virgin or extra virgin olive oil. 'Olive oil' is less expensive and has less flavour and aroma than higher grades of olive oil. The 'olive oil' grade has the same health benefits of the higher quality virgin and extra virgin grades. It just doesn't taste as good. It also has a higher smoke point than virgin or extra virgin oil, making it an excellent choice for cooking. In addition to culinary use, olive oil is also an ingredient in cosmetics, soap and pharmaceuticals.

NUT AND SEED OILS

ALMOND OIL

Like many of the other oils obtained from nuts, almond oil is very expensive, so the demand for it is limited. It has a subtle toasted almond aroma and flavour and is suitable for salad dressings and as an addition to sauces. It is often used in desserts, however, unlike almond extract, almond oil is not concentrated enough to provide a strong almond taste to sweet recipes. It has a high smoke point so it may be used for high heat cooking. Almond oil is a good source of monounsaturated fat and vitamins A and E and is often used as a massage oil or carrier for aromatherapy oils. It is most often available in gourmet shops and in some food stores.

ARGAN OIL

Argan oil is obtained from the nuts grown on argan trees, which are native only to Morocco. Argan trees don't grow in any other area of the world, although efforts are being made to cultivate this variety of tree in other countries. The tree is twisted and gnarled in appearance, with thorny branches yielding a green fruit containing a hard-shelled interior that covers several almond-like nuts. The oil obtained from the nuts is expensive due to the slower traditional methods of production. Twenty to 30 hours of work is required to produce one litre of oil. After processing, the remaining by-product is a deep brown, thick paste referred to as 'amlou', similar to tahini or peanut butter and is most often used as a dip or spread that is served over bread, toast or biscuits.

Argan oil has a golden yellow colour with a slight reddish tint and a pleasing nutty aroma. It provides a smooth, roasted nut flavour somewhat similar to hazelnuts, but with a slightly sharp overtone. It is available in gourmet and speciality shops as well as Middle Eastern markets.

HAZELNUT OIL

Hazelnut oil has a strong, roasted hazelnut flavour and is generally used for baked goods and for some sauces. It is excellent when brushed on fish and it works well as a marinade. This brown-coloured oil can also be added to mildly flavoured oils to create rich-tasting salad dressings.

Hazelnut oil is expensive and it is usually found in gourmet shops, although some grocery stores may have a supply. If it is stored in a cool dark cupboard, it will remain fresh for as long as three months, but it is best to store it in the refrigerator to prevent it from becoming rancid. Hazelnut oil is particularly popular in French cuisine.

MACADAMIA NUT OIL

This is an oil obtained from the nut of the macadamia tree. The tree is native to Australia, which leads the world in production of the nut and the oil. Hawaii, Kenya, South Africa and Guatemala are other major producers. Most  brands of the oil are cold-pressed. The oil has the same rich, buttery flavour as the popular nut and is excellent when used in salads, as a seasoning, or in cooking. The high smoke point makes it a good choice for sautéing and frying.

One of the best features of macadamia nut oil is its nutritional qualities. It contains the highest level of heart-healthy, monounsaturated fat of any edible oil and it has an exact balance of omega-3 and omega-6 fatty acids. The high level of antioxidants slows rancidity and allows the oil to be kept for up to two years without refrigeration.

PEANUT OIL

In the United States, the oil obtained from peanuts is almost clear and has a mild flavour due to the refining process that is used. The Chinese version has more of a peanut taste and aroma. Refined peanut oil has a high smoke point so it is an excellent choice for sautéing and frying. It does not absorb or transfer flavours from food during the cooking process. It is also high in monounsaturated and polyunsaturated fats, which makes it a healthy oil to use for cooking or as a base for dressings. It will keep for long periods if stored in its original container in a cool, dark place.

Since so many people are now allergic to peanuts, there is a worry that peanut oil will cause severe allergic reactions. Research published in the *British Medical Journal* in 1997 has shown that refined peanut oil will not cause allergic reactions for the overwhelming majority of peanut-allergic individuals. Under strict medical surveillance, 60 peanut-allergic adults were fed refined peanut oil and also unrefined (crude) peanut oil. As a result, six of them suffered allergic reactions to the crude oil, but these were only mild. None reacted to the refined oil.

Although the refined oils did not cause dangerous reactions, this may not quite be the whole story. Theoretically, it is possible that traces of peanut protein which cannot cause a reaction would nevertheless sensitise someone, or increase the sensitivity of someone who is already allergic. To find out if this happens, a quite separate research project would be needed, but this might not be practical. It is therefore recommended that if you are allergic to peanuts, you should avoid any peanut oil if possible, but not get too worried if you make a mistake about refined peanut oil

PECAN NUT OIL

Nut oils are often referred to as 'seasoning oils'. Because of their low smoke point, they are not generally used for cooking, but rather to finish dishes. You will nonetheless find recipes written by wonderful and knowledgeable chefs using nut oils for sautéing, dressings and marinades. Pecans, which are grown in the American south, are becoming more popular in Europe. They are sweeter than walnuts and are now being used as an alternative to them.

PISTACHIO NUT OIL

Pistachio nut oil is cold-pressed oil from the fruit of *Pistacia vera*. Pistachio nut oil has a powerful flavour which does not go with everything. Nonetheless, it goes well with both sweet (pastries and fruits) and savoury dishes. In terms of nutritional value, it is high in unsaturated fatty acids, so it is considered a healthy oil.

PUMPKIN SEED OIL

The oil that is pressed from pumpkin seeds is a deep reddish-green colour and has a uniquely delicious taste. Pumpkin seed oil is one of the top three nutritional oils along with hemp seed and flax seed, that provide the best ratio of omega-3 and omega-6. Pumpkin seed oil has a strong flavour and is best used in its raw state, on roasted vegetables or fish, or drizzled into soups. However, it can be combined with milder oils to make it suitable for cooking and salad dressings.

SESAME SEED OIL

The rich, almost odourless oil expressed from these tiny seeds is very stable. If properly stored, sesame seed oil is not likely to go rancid, making it popular as a cooking oil in Indian and Chinese cookery. It is also highly nutritious, rich in vitamins, minerals and omega-3 and omega-6. White sesame seed oil is most common in the West, but in India they say the best oil for healing is extracted from black sesame seeds.

WALNUT OIL

Walnut oil, which is cold-pressed from the meat of dried walnuts, has a strong and distinctive walnut taste. It is generally used as a flavouring for baked goods and for some sauces. It can provide a bold accent to salad dressings or it can be added to mildly flavoured oils to create a more subtle taste. It can be used for sautéing and pan-frying, but the high heat will diminish the impact of the oil and the unrefined version does not have a particularly high smoke point.

Walnut oil is expensive and it is usually found in gourmet shops, although some supermarkets may stock it. Like other oils obtained from nuts, walnut oil is very popular in French cooking.

PLANT AND VEGETABLE OILS

CORN OIL

Corn oil is produced from the germ of corn (maize) and contains over 60% polyunsaturated fat. Refined corn oil is one of the best oils for frying because of its high smoke point. It has a light golden colour and is almost tasteless and odourless, so it is also a good choice for baking. It can be used for salad dressings when oil with little or no taste is required. Corn oil is often a key ingredient in the manufacture of margarine.

COTTONSEED OIL

Cottonseed oil is extracted from the seeds of the cotton plant after the cotton lint has been removed. It contains over 50% omega-6 fatty acids and only trace amounts of omega-3, which is considered an unhealthy balance if not used in moderation. Cottonseed oil is not normally sold retail, but is almost always blended with other oils and it is also used in the manufacture of margarine, salad dressings and commercially prepared fried products.

FLAXSEED OIL

Flaxseed oil is obtained from the seeds of the flax plant. When it is processed, the oil is first cold-pressed from the seeds, which provides an edible oil for use with foods. The seeds are then hot-pressed to produce an industrial oil and solvent, known as linseed oil, which is not edible.

Flaxseed oil has a smooth, buttery flavour, which makes it ideal as a salad oil or as an addition to cooked vegetables and is considered to be one of nature's richest sources of omega-3 fatty acids.

Flaxseed oil also contains vitamins, minerals and approximately 50% more omega-3 than fish oils.

HEMP SEED OIL

There has been a lot of interest in hemp seed oil recently. To most people, *Cannabis sativa* is synonymous with marijuana, but the plant's Latin name means 'useful hemp'. Hemp seed oil has the highest polyunsaturated content of all the oils we are discussing. It is now generally available from gourmet shops and some supermarkets.

MUSTARD SEED OIL

Mustard seed oil is obtained from pressing the mustard seeds from Indian mustard plants, rather than the more common seeds that are found in the Mediterranean. The oil is flavourful, but extremely hot, so it should be used very sparingly as a flavouring ingredient. When cooking with mustard oil, it must be brought to its smoking point before food is cooked in it. When the oil reaches the smoking point, a taste change occurs that results in a smoother mustard flavour, which will not overpower the food.

Mustard oil is widely used in Indian cooking and is a popular addition to salad dressings, stir-fry recipes, and marinades for meat and fish. It is available in Indian and Middle Eastern grocery stores. It will stay fresh for six months or more if it is stored in the refrigerator.

However, a new EU ruling says that all mustard oil must be marked 'for external use only' because the erucic acid content is well above 5% and therefore cannot be classified as a food. It is also not considered suitable for human consumption in either the US or Canada because it is thought that high percentages of erucic acid may be detrimental or toxic. This is not to say that many cooks do not continue to use it for culinary purposes, but one should be aware of the possible risks.

PALM OIL

Palm oil is one of the few plant products that is very high in saturated fat. The oil is obtained from the pulp of the fruit of the African oil palm tree. It has a red-orange colour, a strong unique flavour, and is very popular in the preparation of dishes native to the Caribbean, Central and South America, and Western Africa. A highly refined version of palm oil has very little colour and is usually blended with other oils for the creation of generic vegetable fats and oils.

PALM KERNEL OIL

Palm kernel oil differs from palm oil in that it is extracted from the kernel, rather than the fruit of the palm. It has a light yellow colour and it has a milder flavour than palm oil. Like coconut and palm oils, it is extremely high in saturated fat, but because the saturated fat in the oil is plant-based, some studies suggest that it does not raise low-density lipoprotein (bad) cholesterol in the body (see coconut oil). Palm kernel oil is often used in the manufacture of various cosmetics and in some brands of margarine.

PINE NUT OIL

Pine nut oil is one of the most expensive oils on the market, so its appeal is very limited. It is excellent in salads, as a flavouring, or to dress freshly cooked vegetables. Pine nut oil has a relatively low smoke point, so it is not generally used for cooking.

In Russia, before the 1917 revolution, it was used for cooking during Lent, when the eating of animal fats was forbidden.

Pine nut oil is reportedly an excellent bread preservative, when a small amount is added to the dough before baking.

It has also often been touted as an appetite suppressant.

POPPY SEED OIL

Poppy seed oil is a good choice for salad dressings because of its smooth, subtle flavour. It also works well as a condiment, especially for dipping crusty bread.

RAPESEED OIL

Rapeseed is another of the new 'wonder oils'. Canola is the marketing name in the US and Canada for oil that is obtained from rapeseeds and is genetically modified, unlike European rapeseed oil which is not. Bright yellow rape crops can be spotted (and smelled) in fields in many parts of Britain, Europe and North America. The oil is well-liked in Japan, China and India, and it is the most widely used oil in Canada. It is also popular in the northern United States and is gaining popularity throughout the remainder of the country.

Rapeseed oil contains a very low level of saturated fat and has a high omega-3 fatty acid content. Because it is mildly flavoured, rapeseed oil is an excellent choice for cooking or baking, or as an ingredient for salad dressings. It is just starting to be sold in UK supermarkets.

RICE BRAN OIL

Rice bran oil is produced from the rice bran, which is removed from the grain of rice as it is processed. It is considered to be a very healthy alternative to some other cooking oils because it is rich in vitamins, minerals and omegas. Rice bran oil has a somewhat nutty flavour that enhances the taste of foods when used in processing or preparing snack foods, fried foods and rice crackers.

SOYBEAN OIL

Soybean oil is one of the most widely used oils in the manufacture of margarine, vegetable oil and solid fats. In fact, in the United States, soybean oil is used more often than any other oil in the production of commercially prepared food items. It has long been one of the top favourites for use in Chinese cooking.

Soybean oil is highly refined and has a high smoke point, making it a good all-purpose cooking oil. The generic brands of vegetable oil are often 100% soybean oil, or they may be a blend of several highly refined oils. Soybean oil is inexpensive and has several healthy attributes including high levels of omega-3 and it is fairly low in saturated fat. Soybean oil is used by the food industry in a variety of food products including salad dressings, sandwich spreads, margarine, bread, mayonnaise, non-dairy coffee creamers and snack foods.

SAFFLOWER OIL
The safflower, which is a member of the thistle family, grows to a height of 4 feet and is topped by beautiful yellow, gold and orange flowers. It does well in arid climates due to its long taproot, which may reach 12 feet in length. The seeds of the safflower are used for the production of safflower oil, which has one of the highest levels of polyunsaturated fat of any edible oil. It is low in saturated fat, so it is considered to be a healthy all-purpose oil. However, it contains a low level of monounsaturated fat and contains no vitamin E, so it is not as highly regarded nutritionally as many of the other edible oils. Refined safflower oil is excellent for sautéing, pan-frying and deep-frying because of its very high smoke point. It is also suitable for salad dressings and it can be chilled without solidifying.

SUNFLOWER OIL
Although sunflower seeds are popular as a snack, the oil extracted from the seeds is also commonly used. The seeds of the sunflower are obtained from the brown hub in the centre of the flower, which has yellow petals surrounding it. Sunflower seed oil is a light yellow colour and has a mild flavour. It is suitable for use as a base for salad dressings or in combination with stronger flavoured, more expensive oils. It is also used for cooking because, like most other refined oils, it has a fairly high smoke point.

Although most sunflower oil is obtained through a refining process, there is a small quantity that is now cold-pressed. Like olive oil, the cold-pressed sunflower oil is

known as 'extra virgin', which makes it much more expensive than the refined oil. It also has a better flavour.

TEA OIL

Tea oil is made from tea seeds, which are harvested from the tea plant (*Camilla sinensis*). The seeds are cold-pressed to produce the oil. Pale amber-green in colour, tea oil has a herbal aroma with a somewhat sweet flavour. It is often used in Asian foods and it can be served as a salad dressing when it is combined with other flavours, such as lemon or lime. It can be added to cooked vegetables, pasta, and stir-fry recipes, and can also be used as a base for dips, dressings, marinades and sauces. Tea oil has a high smoke point so it can withstand high heat cooking without burning.

TEA TREE OIL
Tea tree, 'the magic oil', is not an edible oil and shouldn't be confused with tea oil (see Body care and alternative therapies).

VEGETABLE OIL
'Vegetable oil' is a catch-all phrase used for a highly refined blend of various oils such as soybean, corn, palm and sunflower, or it may consist of only one type of oil. The label may or may not list the types of oil contained within the blend, so the consumer will often never know exactly what they are purchasing. The refining process usually results in oil that has a high smoke point and a colour ranging from almost clear to golden-yellow, but with very little taste or aroma. This makes vegetable oil a good all-purpose oil for sautéing, frying and baking, but it should not be used as a condiment or for salad dressings.

FISH OIL
Fish oil is a nutritional supplement not used in cookery (see Body care and alternative therapies). It is recommended for a healthy diet because it contains the omega-3 fatty acids eicosapentaenoic acid (EPA) and docosahexaenoic acid (DHA), that help reduce inflammation throughout the body.

Quick
Reference
Guide

QUICK REFERENCE GUIDE

Type of Oil or Fat	Saturated Fat	Monounsaturated Fat
Almond Oil	8%	73%
Apricot Kernel Oil	6%	64%
Argan Oil	18%	43%
Avocado Oil	20%	70%
Butter	66%	30%
Clarified Butter	65%	32%
Coconut Oil	92%	6%
Corn Oil	13%	25%
Cottonseed Oil	24%	26%
Flaxseed Oil	9%	19%
Grapeseed Oil	12%	17%

Polyunsaturated Fat	Approximate Smoke Point	Main Uses
19%	250°C/495°F	Salad dressing, baking, sauces, desserts, nutritional supplements, massage oil, aromatherapy
30%	250°C/495°F	Cooking, salad dressing, massage oil, aromatherapy
39%	220°C/425°F	Cooking, salad dressing, cosmetics
10%	250°C/495°F	Cooking, salad dressing, flavouring
4%	150°C/300°F	Cooking, baking, sauces, flavouring
3%	190°C/375°F	Deep-frying, cooking, sautéing, flavouring
2%	160°C/325°F	Commercial baked goods, confectionery, non-dairy whipped toppings and coffee creamers, cooking fat
62%	230°C/450°F	Frying, baking, salad dressing, margarine, cooking fat
50%	220°C/425°F	Margarine, cooking fat, salad dressing, commercial fried products
72%	110°C/225°F	Nutritional supplements, salad dressing
71%	200°C/400°F	Cooking, salad dressing, margarine

HEALTHY OILS

Type of Oil or Fat	Saturated Fat	Monounsaturated Fat
Hazelnut Oil	10%	76%
Hemp Seed Oil	8%	12%
Lard	41%	47%
Macadamia Nut Oil	12%	85%
Margarine, hard	70%	14%
Margarine, soft	20%	47%
Mustard Seed Oil	1%	76%
Olive Oil	11%	69%
Virgin Olive Oil	11%	69%
Extra Virgin Olive Oil	11%	69%
Palm Oil	52%	38%
Palm Kernel Oil	82%	11%
Peanut Oil	18%	49%
Pecan Nut Oil	7%	63%

Polyunsaturated Fat	Approximate Smoke Point	Main Uses
14%	220°C/425°F	Salad dressing, baking, flavouring
80%	160°C/325°F	Cooking, salad dressing
12%	175-200°C/ 350-400°F	Baking, frying
3%	190°C/375°F	Cooking, salad dressing, flavouring, marinades, skin care
16%	150-160°C/ 300-325°F	Cooking, baking, flavouring
33%	150-160°C/ 300-325°F	Cooking, baking, flavouring
23%	200°C/400°F	Cooking, flavouring, salad dressing, marinades, massage, animal repellent
20%	190°C/375°F	Cooking, salad dressing, margarine
20%	220°C/425°F	Frying, sautéing, stir-frying, cooking, salad dressing, margarine
20%	220°C/425°F	Cooking, salad dressing, margarine
10%	230°C/450°F	Cooking, flavouring, vegetable oil, cooking fat
7%	Not applicable	Margarine production, cosmetics
33%	230°C/450°F	Frying, cooking, salad dressing, margarine
20%	230°C/450°F	Salad dressing, baking, marinades, flavouring

HEALTHY OILS

Type of Oil or Fat	Saturated Fat	Monounsaturated Fat
Pine Nut Oil	9%	31%
Pistachio Nut Oil	16%	65%
Poppy Seed Oil	14%	21%
Pumpkin Seed Oil	9%	34%
Rapeseed Oil	6%	62%
Rice Bran Oil	19%	42%
Safflower Oil	10%	13%
Sesame Seed Oil	14%	40%
Soybean Oil	15%	24%
Sunflower Oil	11%	20%
Tea Oil	Not available	88%
Tea Tree Oil	Not edible	—
Walnut Oil	14%	19%
Wheatgerm Oil	20%	25%

Polyunsaturated Fat	Approximate Smoke Point	Main Uses
60%	Not applicable	Salad dressing, flavouring
19%	150°C/300°F	Salad dressing, flavouring, massage
65%	Not applicable	Salad dressing, condiment
57%	160°C/325°F	Salad dressing, flavouring, lubricants
32%	230°C/450°F	Frying, baking, salad dressing
39%	250°C/500°F	Cooking, flavouring, commercial snack foods
77%	250°C/500°F	Cooking, salad dressing, margarine
46%	175°C/350°F	Stir-frying, salad dressing, flavouring
61%	230°C/450°F	Cooking, salad dressing, vegetable oil, margarine, cooking fat
69%	230°C/450°F	Cooking, salad dressing, margarine, cooking fat
Not available	250°C/500°F	Stir-frying, salad dressing, sauces and marinades
—	—	Aromatherapy, hair care, skin lotion
67%	160°C/325°F	Salad dressing, flavouring
55%	110°C/225°F	Salad dressing, flavouring

Our Ancestors Were Pretty Smart

History of Edible Oils

OLIVE OIL

No oil has had a greater impact on history than olive oil.

The olive has a very old and sacred background.
Fossilized remains of the olive tree's ancestor were found
near Livorno, Italy, dating from 20 million years ago,
although actual cultivation probably did not occur in that
area until 500 BC.

No one can actually prove where olives were first
cultivated. The Greeks maintain it was in Crete *circa*
5000-3500 BC and that from there, olive cultivation spread
to Syria, Palestine and Israel, and then to Southern
Turkey, Cyprus, and Egypt. Others say the cultivated olive
tree originated in Asia Minor, between present day Syria
and Iran. Still other theories state that cultivation may

have started in the Phoenician colonies of the present territories of Palestine and Lebanon, much closer to the Mediterranean, at the beginning of the Neolithic period around the year 6000 BC.

Whatever the truth is, olives and their oil played a major part in the Bible and ancient history. An olive tree branch appears at the sarcophagus of some pharaohs, like Tutankhamun.

The Bible contains many references to the culinary and religious uses of olives and olive oil. In the Book of Genesis, the dove sent out from the ark by Noah returned with an olive branch. Here it became the great symbol of peace, indicating the end of God's anger. And its recognition by Noah suggests that it was already a well-known tree.

In Hellenic society, olive trees were considered so sacred that those who cut one down were condemned to death or exile. In olden Greece and Rome, olive oil was a hot commodity; ships were built for the sole purpose of transporting it from Greece to trading posts around the Mediterranean.

The belief that olive oil conferred strength and youth was widespread. In ancient Egypt, Greece and Rome, it was infused with flowers and grasses to produce both medicine and cosmetics; a list was excavated in Mycenae enumerating the aromatics (fennel, sesame, celery, watercress, mint, sage, rose and juniper among others) added to olive oil in the preparation of ointments.

The symbolic meaning of the olive tree, as well as the exceptional value of olive oil, is visible in overall sectors of ancient Greece's life. A number of facts show us the relationship between the olive tree and its product with some social activities. It is characteristic that when the first Olympic Games took place in Olympia in 776 BC an olive tree branch symbolising peace was the award to the winners. In addition, the winners also received olive oil. The quantities were huge. Depending on the sport, the top winner could take home a quantity of about 5 tons.

Obviously this amount could not be consumed by the winner himself, so it is easy to imagine how rich some of these athletes became. (Nothing changes in professional sports!)

The 'golden age' of the olive grove coincides with the Roman period from 300 BC until AD 200.

The Roman Empire spread civilisation and the cultivation of olive groves throughout southern Europe. Indeed, the importance of olive oil was so great that the Empire's southern regions were organised around oil provinces. When the Roman Empire collapsed, the cultivation of olive groves fell into disfavour and for hundreds of years olives survived only in a few fortified regions high in the hills of Tuscany.

Around AD 1100, olive groves began to flourish in Italy once again and Tuscany became a renowned region of cultivation of the olive tree. Some of the strict laws issued during that time, regulating the cultivation of olives and the commerce of oil, are still followed today. By 1400, Italy had become the greatest producer of olive oil in the world, offering extraordinary oil that graced Renaissance tables across Europe. And while olive oil production slowed briefly during the late 1600s due to taxation issues, in the long run it continued to grow through the centuries as civilisation spread around the globe.

The expansion of the olive tree in the New World was undertaken by the Spanish Conquistadors from the beginning of the 16th century. At first it was introduced in the Antilles and afterwards in the American continent. Mexico had olive groves in regular production towards the end of the 16th century. From here, they expanded to Peru and then to Chile. At about the same time, the plant was introduced in Argentina where it adapted perfectly well.

Franciscan missionaries brought the first olive trees to the United States, specifically California, in the 18th century, when it was introduced by Fra Junípero Serra, founder of the San Diego de Alcalá mission. Years later, olive trees were planted by Franciscan fathers in the missions they established along the 600 miles of the Californian coast. Presently, the olive tree variety called 'mission' is related to those foundations.

One hundred years later, olive oil made its commercial debut in the Americas as Italian and Greek immigrants began demanding its import from Europe. Initially an ethnic speciality, olive oil was soon embraced by mainstream American cooks.

The great British cookery writer, Elizabeth David, published *Mediterranean Food* in 1950, when Britain was still in the throes of rationing. At that time no one cooked recipes from this book because the exotic ingredients were unknown and unavailable.

'Vegetable' was the oil of 1970s Britain. British shoppers knew olive oil best as a dissolver of ear wax, and it was sold for that purpose in small bottles by chemists.

Until 20 years ago, olive oil was an obscure epicurean product in the UK, bought from delicatessens by homesick southern Europeans and devotees of Elizabeth David. Aided by the new popularity of Italian cooking and its comparative healthiness, olive oil snuck into our larders. And we like it more and more every year.

In the late 20th century, American scientists published several nutritional articles citing a marked correlation between the so-called 'Mediterranean Diet' and lower incidences of health problems. Based on fresh vegetables, seasonal fruits, grains, fish, meats and olive oil, the studies confirmed that foods of the Mediterranean region aren't just delicious; they are also a smart choice for good health.

Now, in the 21st century, olive oil continues to grow in popularity and plays a part in cuisines of virtually every culture. There are over 800 million olive trees in the world with more being planted every day.

The countries surrounding the Mediterranean produce more than 90% of the world's olive oil, with Italy, Spain and Greece dominating the market. No two olive oils are alike. Each is a unique product of soil, climate, olive varieties, age and processing methods. Oils can be fruity or flowery, nutty or spicy, delicate or mild, and can range from clear to pale green, to golden, to deep olive green in colour. When properly processed, olive oil can fully maintain the flavour, aroma and vitamins of the eloquent olive from which it came.

OTHER IMPORTANT CULINARY OILS

ALMOND OIL
The almond tree is a native of the warmer parts of Western Asia and North Africa, but it has been extensively distributed over the warm temperate region of the Old World and is cultivated in all the countries bordering the Mediterranean. It was introduced into England probably by the Romans and occurs in the Anglo-Saxon lists of plants, but was not cultivated in the UK until after the mid-16th century and then chiefly for its blossom.

However, almonds, as well as the oil pressed from them, were well-known in Greece and Italy long before the Christian era. In ancient times oils were highly desirable for cooking, lighting, medicine, and for perfumes. Almond oil from Anatolia, now Turkey, was a sought-after commodity in Greece. And here's a bit of trivia — in the US almond oil has been used as a lubricant for fine watches.

APRICOT KERNEL OIL
It is believed that apricots originated in China. From there, they were brought westward and introduced into Asia Minor and Europe. Spanish explorers are credited for introducing the apricot to the North American continent; specifically California, where they were planted in the gardens of Spanish missions.

ARGAN OIL
The argan tree, which grows only in south-western Morocco, is believed to date back 25 million years. Its history is tied closely to

the history of the Berber people. For hundreds of years they have used it as a source of fuel and building material. It has also been used as a traditional medicine and a dietary staple — usually eaten on bread or in 'amlou', a sweet oil and almond paste, regarded as an aphrodisiac. Now endangered and under the protection of the United Nations, the argan tree flourishes in sandy soil at the edge of the Sahara Desert.

AVOCADO OIL

The avocado or avocado pear is native to Central and South America. The earliest record of its existence was an archaeological dig in Peru that uncovered avocado seeds buried with a mummy and dated back to the 8th century BC. One theory was that these early people wanted the seeds buried with them because their aphrodisiac qualities might be useful in the afterlife!

When Hernando Cortez conquered Mexico in 1519, he found that the avocado was a staple in the native diet. The Conquistadors discovered a unique use for the avocado seed. The seed yields a milky liquid that becomes red when exposed to air. The Spaniards found they could use this reddish-brown or even blackish indelible liquid as ink to be used on documents. Some of these documents are still in existence today.

In the 1700s English seamen discovered that the avocado could be used as a spread to soften the hardtack they had for meals. This avocado spread soon became known as 'midshipman's butter'.

While the fruit of the avocado has been enjoyed by many cultures throughout the centuries, Australian and New Zealand avocado farmers and imaginative food professionals invented a new oil at the beginning of this century, cold-pressed from the fruit. Avocados are grown in many countries, but the idea of extracting oil from this popular fruit is definitely new and becoming very trendy.

COCONUT OIL

Coconut oil has been used for centuries as a vital source of food for health and general well-being in the tropics.

It is one of the oldest recorded sources of vegetable oil and is still cultivated and used for cooking in those regions.

Once a highly valued, worldwide commodity for cooking, coconut oil was eventually replaced by soybean, peanut and cottonseed oils. However, the oil is gaining recognition in the US and Europe for its health benefits. Recent research verifies traditional beliefs that the coconut palm is 'The Tree of Life' and that, just like any other pure, whole food, coconuts and virgin coconut oil have a significant role to play in a well-balanced, nutritious diet.

Some historians believe coconuts were brought to the tropical regions where coconuts presently grow by explorers and sea travellers.

Coconuts made a strong impression on Venetian explorer Marco Polo when he encountered them in Sumatra, India and the Nicobar Islands, calling them 'Pharaoh's nut'. The reference to the Egyptian ruler indicated Polo was aware that during the 6th century Arab merchants brought coconuts back to Egypt probably from East Africa where the nuts were flourishing.

Had it not been for the curiosity of a nobleman from Venice who decided to explore the world as a tourist, Ferdinand Magellan's voyage from Spain in 1519 might have gone unrecorded. Antonio Pigafetta boarded one of Magellan's five ships and kept a daily journal of his captain's effort to find a western route to the Spice Islands.

Magellan encountered a host of troubles, mainly scurvy and

starvation. A last resort decision to go ashore when they spotted the island of Guam brought them more troubles. Unfriendly natives wearing coconut shell masks and shaking coconut shell rattles with human bone handles greeted them on the shore. Magellan was able to negotiate and came away with provisions and a good supply of coconuts.

Pigafetta wrote:

> *Coconuts are the fruit of the palm trees. And as we have bread, wine, oil, and vinegar, so they get all these things from the said trees . . . With two of these palm trees a whole family of ten can sustain itself . . . They last for a hundred years.*

Not long after Magellan's voyage, Sir Francis Drake journeyed from England to the Cape Verde Islands off Africa's West Coast in 1577. He, too, was impressed with coconuts and wrote:

> *Amongst other things we found here a kind of fruit called Cocos, which because it is not commonly known with us in England, I thought good to make some description of it.*

Though the accounts of many explorers mention coconuts, the nuts remained unknown outside their tropical habitats until 1831 when J.W. Bennett, an Englishman, wrote *A Treatise on the Coco-nut Tree and the Many Valuable Properties Possessed by the Splendid Palm*. Revelations such as applying charcoal from the shell as a tooth cleanser, removing wrinkles with coconut water, and using the root for medicinal purposes spurred European interest in the nut.

From past centuries to the present, the nuts are considered survival food, sustaining communities after major tropical storms destroy the rice paddies or corn fields. Coconuts come to market in two major stages of maturity. Young coconuts are prized for their sweet, revitalising juice. The meat of the young coconut, which is very thin, soft and delicately sweet, is gaining interest among innovative raw foodies who turn it into imitation noodles and other delicacies.

The mature coconut is valued for its thick, firm meat used worldwide in shredded or grated form, often for baked goods. Coconut in its mature stage has a rich, nutty flavour and chewy texture with a higher oil content than young coconut. Coconut milk, coconut cream and coconut oil all come from mature coconuts.

CORN OIL

Corn refining began in the United States around the time of the Civil War. The first product was cornstarch (cornflour). A bit later, corn was discovered to yield sugar (dextrose) from the starch. Around the same time, the industry also began to realise the value of the non-starch parts of corn. Fibre, germ and protein from the corn had simply been discarded until manufacturers discovered they could turn them into valuable animal feed ingredients. The industry then discovered that corn oil could be extracted from the germ. The first commercial production of corn oil took place in 1889.

COTTONSEED OIL

While olive oil and other pressed oils have been around for millennia, Procter & Gamble researchers in America were innovators when they started selling cottonseed oil as a solid cooking fat in 1911. Ginning mills were happy to have someone haul away the cotton seeds. P & G learned how to extract the oil, refine it, partially hydrogenate it (causing it to be solid at room temperature and thus mimic natural lard). Compared with the rendered lard P & G was already selling to consumers, Crisco, the brand name, was cheaper, easier to stir into a recipe, and could be stored at room temperature for two years without turning rancid.

FLAXSEED OIL

Flaxseeds have a long and extensive history. Originating in Mesopotamia, the flax plant has been known since the Stone Age. One of the first records of the culinary use of flaxseeds goes back to ancient Greece. In both that civilisation and in ancient Rome, the health benefits of flaxseeds were widely praised. After the fall of Rome, the cultivation and popularity of flaxseeds declined.

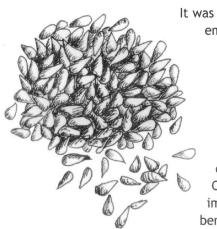

It was Charlemagne, the emperor who would be famous for shaping European history, who also helped to shape the history of flaxseeds, restoring them to their noble position in the food culture of Europe. Charlemagne was so impressed with how beneficial flax was in terms of its culinary, medicinal, and fibre usefulness (flaxseed fibres can be woven into linen) that he passed laws requiring not only its cultivation, but its consumption as well. After Charlemagne, flaxseeds became widely appreciated throughout Europe.

It was not until the early colonists arrived in North America that flax was first planted in the United States. In the 17th century, flax was introduced and planted in Canada, the country that is currently the major producer of this extremely beneficial seed.

GRAPESEED OIL

Although known to Europeans for centuries, grapeseed oil was not produced or used on a large scale until the 20th century, largely due to the fact that grape seeds contain a lower percentage of oil compared with other oil-producing seeds, nuts or beans.

HAZELNUT OIL

Hazelnuts date back to ancient times. Old Chinese manuscripts indicate their use is as old as agricultural history, going back nearly 5,000 years. Hazelnut culture was known to the ancient Greeks and Romans, and the nuts were thought to have medicinal qualities in addition to their food value.

Hazelnuts are grown in many countries and are now considered the world's second most plentiful nut.

HEMP SEED OIL

Hemp is another word for the plant *Cannabis sativa L.* Marijuana comes from this same plant genus — and so do broccoli and cauliflower. But the strains of hemp used in industrial and consumer products contain only a negligible level of the intoxicating substance delta-9 tetrahydrocannabinol, or THC. Thus, industrial grade hemp is *not* marijuana.

Hemp has been grown for the last 12,000 years for fibre (textiles and paper) and food. It has been effectively prohibited in the United States since the 1950s. But it was not always so.

In 1619, America's first marijuana law was enacted at Jamestown Colony, Virginia, 'ordering' all farmers to 'make tryal of' (grow) Indian hemp seed. More mandatory hemp cultivation laws were enacted in Massachusetts in

1631, in Connecticut in 1632 and in the Chesapeake Colonies into the mid-1700s.

Even in England, the much-sought-after prize of full British citizenship was bestowed by a decree of the crown on foreigners who would grow cannabis, and fines were often levied against those who refused. Hemp was once grown by every farmer in Britain under orders from Elizabeth I when it was needed to make rope for the navy.

Cannabis hemp was legal tender in most of the Americas from 1631 until the early 1800s. Why? To encourage American farmers to grow more.

You could pay your taxes with cannabis hemp throughout America for over 200 years.

You could even be jailed in America for not growing cannabis during several periods of shortage.

George Washington and Thomas Jefferson both grew hemp on their plantations. Ben Franklin owned a mill that made hemp paper. Jefferson drafted the Declaration of Independence on hemp paper.

Today hemp is staging a comeback, used by fashion designers and mass producers alike. In addition to established producers such as China, Romania, Hungary and France, hemp crops are now also grown in Australia, Canada, Britain and Germany where for decades there had been none. It is legally cultivated in at least 30 countries around the world, including every G-8 country. Even in the US an experimental crop is being grown in Hawaii under a government licence.

MACADAMIA NUT OIL
The macadamia nut was discovered by British colonists in Queensland, Australia in 1857. Walter Hill, who was the Director of the Botany Garden in Brisbane, found one of the nuts, cracked it open using a vice and planted the seed. This 'first' macadamia nut tree is still growing and producing nuts, although typically the trees only produce for about 70 years.

The tree was named after Scotsman John Macadam, a friend, physician, and member of the Philosophical Institute of Victoria. Mr Macadam never tasted the nut that bears his name after a shipboard injury caused his premature death en route to New Zealand. The macadamia migrated to Hawaii courtesy of William Herbert Purvis who gathered macadamia nuts near Mount Bauple in Queensland, Australia, and brought them to Hawaii's Big Island in 1882.

Of course, the trees had long been known to the native Australian aborigines who called the macadamia trees *kindal kindal* and who feasted on the nuts in winter.

Macadamia nuts have the hardest shells to crack (although they are followed closely by the Brazil nut). The process of cracking the nuts also makes them rare and expensive. Today, in addition to the much-prized nuts, the kernels are ground and processed to produce macadamia nut oil, which has many culinary uses.

PALM OIL

The history of palm oil can be traced back to the days of the Egyptian pharaohs 5,000 years BC. The oil palm tree, however, is a native of West Africa. Among West African peoples it is in widespread use as a cooking oil.

European merchants trading with West Africa occasionally purchased palm oil for use in Europe, but as the oil was bulky and cheap and due to the much higher profits available from slave-trading, palm oil remained rare outside West Africa. During the early 19th century, the decline of the Atlantic slave trade and Europe's demand for legitimate commerce (trade in material goods rather than human lives) obliged African countries to seek new sources of trade revenue. In the Asante Confederacy, state-owned slaves built large plantations of oil palm trees, while in the neighbouring Kingdom of Dahomey, King Ghezo passed a law in 1856 forbidding his subjects from cutting down oil palms. Palm oil became a highly sought-after commodity by British traders, the oil being used as industrial lubricant for the machines of Britain's ongoing Industrial Revolution, as well as forming the basis for different brands of soap, such as Palmolive (manufactured from palm and olive oils).

By around 1870, palm oil constituted the primary export of some West African countries such as Ghana and Nigeria. By the 1880s cocoa had become more highly sought after, leading to the decline of the palm oil industry and trade within these countries. It was introduced to Malaysia at the start of the 20th century and commercially produced in 1917. Today Malaysia's oil palm plantations cover 40% of its cultivated land, and it has become the world's largest producer and exporter of palm oil. Indonesia has also embarked on a massive oil palm plantation programme, and having a much bigger land base, it is expected to catch up soon with Malaysia.

Palm oil has become one of the world's biggest traded commodities and is often the unidentified 'vegetable oil' used in many products from chocolate to cosmetics to animal feed. Because of the high demand, Indonesian and Malaysian growers have destroyed large areas of rainforest to make room for palm oil production. There is a strong movement from environmentalists to force supermarket chains and cosmetic retailers to source only from sustainable growth areas.

In the food industries, palm oil is the choice for manufacturing solid fat products. Palm oil olein and stearin are popularly used worldwide in making margarine, shortenings and confectionery and in frying snack foods.

PEANUT OIL
The peanut, better known worldwide as groundnut and to a lesser extent as earthnut, monkey nut and goober, is not a true nut, but an annual legume much like the bean or pea. The peanut plant is unusual because it flowers

above ground and pods containing one to five seeds are produced underground. Its seeds are a rich source of edible oils and contain 40–50% fat, 20–50% protein, and 10–20% carbohydrate. Peanuts, peanut oil and peanut protein meals constitute an important segment of world trade in oilseeds and products. Peanut is the fifth most important oilseed in the world.

The archaeological records support its cultivation between 300 and 2500 BC. in Peruvian desert oases. Although no archaeological evidence of peanuts has been uncovered in the area due to its tropical climate, the Gurarani region of Paraguay, eastern Bolivia and central Bolivia showed the greatest diversity of wild varieties of peanut species. The cultivated peanut was probably first domesticated in the valleys of the Paraguay and Parana rivers in the Chaco region of South America by predecessors of the Arawak-speaking people who now live there.

The first written account of the crop is found with the Spanish entry into Hispaniola in 1502, where the Arawak cultivated it under the name of mani. Records from Brazil around 1550 show the crop was known there with the name mandubi. Early Spanish and Portuguese accounts record the presence of peanut crop throughout the West Indies and South America.

Today, groundnut is widely distributed and has adapted in various countries of the world. The most important countries for production are India, China, US, West and Southern Africa and Brazil. It is usually divided into four varieties: 'Virginia', 'Peruvian', 'Spanish' and 'Valencia'.

The Virginia variety was taken from the Antilles to Mexico soon after 1500 and then quickly introduced to West Africa. It was brought to eastern North America from both the West Indies and West Africa in the 17th century. The Peruvian variety was taken to the Philippines by Spanish galleons and from there to Southeast China before 1600, where it was known as 'foreign beans'. It spread from there throughout China and to Japan where it was known as 'Chinese beans'. Chinese settlers were probably responsible for introduction to the rest of Southeast Asia and Indonesia. Peanuts arrived in India most likely from Africa, as one of the plant's Indian names was 'Mozambique bean'.

The 'Spanish' groundnut was almost certainly taken from Brazil to Africa by the Portuguese shortly after their contact with Brazil in 1500. There it mixed with 'Virginia' and produced the great diversity of African crops. The 'Spanish' crop was introduced into Spain in the late 18th century, from Brazil via Lisbon. From Spain it travelled to Southern France and finally to the US in 1871. The 'Valencia' was probably introduced to Spain from Cordoba, Argentina about 1900 and was introduced to the US about 1910.

Peanuts did not reach England and France until long after the Spanish and Portuguese had first encountered them.

The peanut is one of the world's most popular and universal crops, cultivated in more than 100 countries in all six continents. China and India are the largest producers. Although the US had been third largest producer in the world until the mid-1990s, Nigeria has now surpassed it.

PECAN NUT OIL
The pecan tree, which is a kinsman of the hickory and walnut family, was growing wild in the United States long before any newcomers arrived there. Though pecan trees grow mostly throughout the Southeastern US today, some historians describe the region surrounding the Mississippi River Basin as the homeland of the pecan; others claim the state of Texas is its place of origin.

Texas may indeed be where the pecan laid its first claim in the US, considering that there are over 70 million wild pecan trees in Texas, and that Texans have been consuming voluminous quantities of pecans since the state was inhabited.

The hickory tree, which is in the pecan family, was growing wild in North America when the first humans crossed the Bering Strait from Asia before 8000 BC. Those first inhabitants were hunter-gatherers and collected the nuts in autumn for winter sustenance along with walnuts and a variety of berries.

Native Americans learned how to use the fruits of the earth for their subsistence and relied on pecans as an important food staple. The early colonists learned survival lessons from the Indians, who shared their knowledge and taught the early settlers how to gather and utilise the nuts for sustenance throughout the harsh winters.

Commercial cultivation of pecans began in the early 1800s but didn't become a major business until the end of the century. Though pecans are popular in the US, Canada and Mexico, they have never achieved world notice. Pecans didn't reach Europe until the 1700s and were shown little enthusiasm. Today, they are grown on a small scale in Israel, New South Wales, Australia, and Natal in South Africa. Australia began harvesting its first good crop in 1960, while Israel's harvesting began in the 1970s.

PINE NUT OIL
Pine nut oil, also called pine seed oil or cedar nut oil, is a pressed vegetable oil, extracted from the edible seeds of several species of pine.

Pine nut oil has a history of many centuries of therapeutic use in Russian and Chinese traditional medicine. The native people of Siberia — a remote region of Russia famous for its pristine forests, crystal-clear rivers and lakes, as well as the remarkably vibrant health of its inhabitants — have always used pine nut oil as an effective, all-natural hunger suppressant, metabolism enhancer, digestive aid and peptic ulcer healer.

PISTACHIO NUT OIL

Pistachio nut oil is a pressed oil, extracted from the fruit of the pistachio nut. Compared to other nut oils, it has a particularly strong flavour. Like other nut oils, it tastes similar to the nut from which it is extracted. The oil is also used for its highly emollient and skin softening qualities.

The first archaeological findings date back to 6760 BC in the Palaeozoic period in the territory of the present Jordan. Although pistachio trees have been known for a long period of time, the place of their origin is uncertain. They probably come from the Middle East, Persia (Iran), and western Asia (eastern Pakistan and India), where they used to grow wild in high-positioned desert regions.

Pistachios were brought to Italy from Syria during the reign of Tiberius at the beginning of the 1st century AD. Subsequently they were grown in other southern European countries. Pistachios were known by the Assyrians and the Greeks as a medicinal drug, a potent aphrodisiac and as an antidote against bites by poisonous animals!

Their commercial use began in the 1930s when businessmen from Iran started to export pistachios to Europe and the US, and also to Czechoslovakia before World War II.

Iran is not only a grower of first-class pistachios, but it is also the main producer of this product in the world, with production reaching well over 100,000 tons annually.

PUMPKIN SEED OIL

Pumpkin seed oil, also called 'the Green Gold', has an old history which began with Christopher Columbus's voyages. Pumpkins and other squashes were New World finds that Columbus's returning ships brought back to Europe. Pumpkins were first used as staple foods for animals and field hands. Later, pressed oil from the

pumpkin seeds was used both in cooking and medicinally — in salves, creams and other healing balms.

After America was 'discovered', the pumpkin was imported to Europe and Asia, where it is still a popular food vegetable. However, the extraction of pumpkin seed oil out of a mutant pumpkin with non-stringy seeds started a long time later.

During the 18th century some knew about the usability of the pumpkin seed. A reference book from 1739 stated: 'it is used often for making cooling emulsions and milks, also other drinks and soups. It is pressed, a white sweet oil out of it which makes a smooth skin . . .' Three years later, a last will document mentioned the heritage of 14 pounds of pumpkin seed oil in the Styrian village of Rassach.

Allegedly, in 1773 the Austrian Empress Maria Theresa ordered that pumpkin seed oil should not serve as a normal food, but belong instead to chemist shops to produce 'ointments and plasters'.

According to some records from the beginning of the 18th century, not only was pumpkin seed oil used for culinary and health purposes, but also for military usage, namely as a lubricant. The polyunsaturated fatty acids in pumpkin seed oil are still the basic materials for lubricants today.

Before World War I pumpkin seed oil was not produced commercially, but was used only by the farmers who grew it. With growing industrialisation, the first hydraulic oil presses were developed.

Today, more than 2,000 tons of Styrian pumpkin seed oil are produced in Austria annually, believed to be the only production site in the world. This top-quality pumpkin seed oil is now distributed globally. Other types of pumpkin seed oil are also marketed worldwide by online shops. International producers use white seeds with shells and this produces a cheaper white oil. New producers of this type of pumpkin seed oil are located in China and India.

RAPESEED OIL

Far from being an overnight wonder, rapeseed has been a part of some cultures for thousands of years. Ancient civilisations in Asia and Europe used rapeseed oil in lamps. Later it was used in foods and as cooking oil. Although the crop was grown in Europe in the 13th century, its use was not extensive until the development of steam power when it was found that rapeseed oil would cling to water and steam-washed metal surfaces better than any other lubricant. In fact, the need for Canadian rapeseed production arose from the critical shortage of the oil that followed the World War II blockage of European and Asian sources in the early 1940s. The oil was urgently needed as a lubricant for the steam engines in naval and merchant ships.

The first edible rapeseed was developed in Canada in 1956. Because the word 'rape' was not considered suitable for marketing, they coined the name 'canola' (from 'Canada Oil') and 'canola' was registered as a name for this crop in the late 1970s. Canola was developed by genetically altering rapeseed to reduce the levels of glucosinolates (which contribute to the sharp taste in mustard) and erucic acid (a fatty acid not essential for human growth). In 1985 the US Food and Drug Administration declared canola 'Generally Recognized as Safe' (GRAS).

Until recently, rapeseed was a relatively unimportant crop. But it is becoming more and more popular. In Canada GM rapeseed has become widespread and canola oil is very popular as a cooking medium in all of North America.

Rapeseed in Europe is not genetically modified. Britain is a latecomer to the cultivation of rapeseed; however, no crop dominates the British arable landscape quite like rapeseed does today.

The main use of the oil-rich rapeseed crop is for the manufacture of cooking oils, margarine and processed foods, with much of the by-product used as animal feed. Globally, rapeseed is the third most important source of cooking oils. A couple of bold UK farmers are seeking to produce a high-quality, extra virgin GM-free rapeseed oil from their crops for domestic use. Their oils have a distinctive nutty flavour, a far cry from the anonymous cooking oil most rapeseed goes to make.

SAFFLOWER OIL
Safflower is a relatively minor oil in the world fats and oils trade, but it has an interesting history. Although safflower is now recognised primarily as a source of healthy edible oil, its traditional uses have not focused on the oil. Rather, safflower was originally valued for the yellow and red dyes yielded by its flowers. These dyes had been used for centuries to colour cosmetics and fabrics. The use of safflower extract to dye the wrappings of mummies has been reported. Safflower had been used as a replacement for saffron, but lost its popularity because of its lack of taste. Traditional uses of safflower tea included inducing sweating and reducing fever. The oil has also been used as a solvent in paints.

SESAME SEED OIL
Many generations ago, in the Middle East where civilisation began and the art of culinary creation was

born, sesame seed oil was discovered. Because of its excellent fragrance, aroma, and ease of cultivation, it could have been the first vegetable oil, perhaps centuries ahead of olive oil. Sesame is one of the oldest known plants in the world. The tiny seeds of sesame have been known as a highly prized source of food oil in Babylon, Assyria and many other Eastern countries for at least 4,000 years. Sesame oil was first referred to in the 6th century as 'Moa' in Chinese and 'Koba' in Japanese. Sesame seed oil is still the main source of fat used in cooking in the Near and Far East.

SOYBEAN OIL

As early as 5,000 years ago, farmers in China grew soybeans. In 1804, a Yankee clipper ship from China brought soybeans to the US. And in 1829, US farmers started growing soybeans. During the American Civil War, soldiers used soybeans as 'coffee berries' to brew 'coffee' when real coffee was scarce. In the late 1800s, significant numbers of farmers began to grow soybeans as forage for cattle. In 1904 in Tuskegee, Alabama, George Washington Carver began studying the soybean. His discoveries changed the way people thought about the soybean; no longer was it just a forage crop. Now its beans provided valuable protein and oil.

By 1929, US soybean production had grown to 9 million bushels (over 240,000 tons). That year, soybean pioneer William J. Morse left on a two-year odyssey to China during which time he gathered many soybean varieties for US researchers to study. Some of these varieties laid the foundation for the rapid ascension of the US as the world leader in soybean production.

Before World War II, the US imported 40% of its edible fats and oils. At the start of the war, this oil supply was cut. American processors turned to soybean oil for their supply. By 1940, the US soybean crop had grown to 78 million bushels (over 2.1 million tons) harvested on 5 million acres.

The US soybean industry began to look at ways to expand export markets. In 1956, the American Soybean

Association in co-operation with the USDA-Foreign Agricultural Service opened its first international office in Japan. Today, it promotes US soybean and soy product exports in more than 80 countries.

By the 1960s, a small but growing livestock industry in Japan began to use soybean meal as a protein and energy source. Rather than pay relatively higher ocean freight costs for the meal and soybean oil, a Japanese soy processing industry began to expand with imports of whole soybeans from the US.

Soybean use in Europe grew slowly in the 1960s and 1970s, but by the 1980s demand for soy meal and soy oil pushed growth in processing capacity.

Between 1976 and 2005, soybean plantings in the US increased by 50% and national average soybean yields increased almost as much. Yield growth is attributed to improved seed varieties, new agronomic practices and the impact of biotechnology-enhanced seeds that are tolerant of key herbicides.

One characteristic of developing economies is that consumer demand for meat and poultry goes up as the population benefits from economic growth. So in the 1980s and 1990s, meat and poultry consumption in countries like China, South Korea, Mexico, Indonesia, Turkey and the Philippines climbed. Demand for soybean products and capacity to produce them soared as well. Now, a thriving soybean processing industry has arisen throughout Asia and has spread to the Middle East, North Africa and throughout the Americas.

The use of soybean products for feed and food has continued to expand worldwide. China quadrupled its soybean processing capacity in just five years, beginning in 1998. Recent years have seen the increases in world soybean production and world soybean demand keep pace with one another. Since the early 1990s, the US share of world soybean production has declined from about 50% to less than 40%. During that time, Brazil's share increased to more than 25%.

Today, soybean oil — together with palm oil — accounts for over half of all oil consumed in the world. And it has been suggested by market analysts that US production of major crude vegetable oils is slated to reach 8.6 million tons in 2008, with soybean oil accounting for nearly 87% of the major vegetable oil production at 7.4 million tons.

SUNFLOWER OIL

The wild sunflower is native to North America, but commercialisation of the plant took place in Russia. It was only recently that the sunflower plant returned to North America to become a cultivated crop. But it was the Native American tribes who first domesticated the sunflower into a single-headed plant with a variety of seed colours.

Evidence suggests that the plant was cultivated by native tribes in present-day Arizona and New Mexico. Some archaeologists suggest that sunflower may have been domesticated before corn.

Sunflower was used in many ways throughout the various tribes. Seed was ground or pounded into flour for cakes, mush or bread. Some tribes mixed the meal with other vegetables such as beans, squash and corn. The seed was also cracked and eaten for a snack. There are references to squeezing the oil from the seed and using the oil in making bread.

Non-food uses include purple dye for textiles, body painting and other decorations. Parts of the plant were used medicinally ranging from snake bite remedies to other body ointments. The oil of the seed was used on the skin and hair. The dried stalk was used as a building material. The plant and the seeds were widely used in ceremonies.

This exotic North American plant was taken to Europe by Spanish explorers some time around 1500. The plant became widespread throughout present-day Western Europe mainly as an ornamental, but some medicinal uses were developed. By 1716, an English patent had been granted for squeezing oil from sunflower seed.

Sunflower became very popular as a cultivated plant in the 18th century. Most of the credit is given to Peter the Great. Although initially used as an ornamental, by 1830, the manufacture of sunflower oil was done on a commercial scale. The Russian Orthodox Church increased its popularity by forbidding most oil foods from being consumed during Lent. However, sunflower was not on the prohibited list and therefore gained in immediate popularity as a food.

By the late 19th century, Russian sunflower seed found its way into the US. The first commercial use of the sunflower crop in the US was as silage feed for poultry. In 1926, the Missouri Sunflower Growers' Association participated in what is likely the first processing of sunflower seed into oil.

Canada started the first official government sunflower growing programme in 1930. Acreage spread because of oil demand. By 1946, Canadian farmers had built a small crushing plant. In 1964, the Government of Canada licensed a Russian variety of sunflower whose seed produced high yields of oil.

There was strong European demand for sunflower oil, stimulated by Russian exports of the oil in previous decades. However, the Russians could no longer supply the growing demand, and European companies looked to the fledgling US industry. Europeans imported sunflower seed that was then crushed in European mills. Western

Europe continues to be a large consumer of sunflower oil today, but depends on its own production.

WALNUT OIL
The first historical accounts of walnut trees growing under civilised cultivation was in ancient Babylon (Iraq) about 2000 BC; however, excavations of cave fossils suggest that walnuts have been around much longer. It is said that the Egyptians used walnut kernel oil to embalm mummies by replacing the blood with walnut oil.
The walnut has its origins in Eastern Europe, Asia Minor, and points eastward to the Himalayan Mountains. However, there are native walnuts in North, Central and South America, Europe and Asia. The ancient Greeks also grew walnuts, but it may have actually been the Persians who first cultivated a superior variety. The walnuts growing in Greece were small and didn't produce a significant quantity of oil. When the Greeks encountered the better Persian walnuts, they began to improve their

crops. The ancient Greeks utilised the walnut not only for food, but also as a medicine and dye for hair and cloth. Romans spread cultivation throughout southern Europe. The species came to the New World with English settlers and to California via missionaries. Today, walnut production is almost entirely located in the San Joaquin/Sacramento valleys of California, where over 5,000 growers and 52 processors make up a highly organised and productive industry.

Good Fats, Bad Fats and Omegas

GOOD FATS, BAD FATS AND OMEGAS

Many people have been so brainwashed by the fat-free mentality of the last decade that they still have a phobia about eating fat. But the idea that all fats are 'bad' is just wrong. There are certainly some fats one should stay away from. While all oils are pure fat, not all fats are created equal. Saturated and trans-fatty acids seem to be the culprits. Read food labels. If it says 'hydrogenated' or 'partially hydrogenated', try to avoid them. Look for fats labelled monounsaturated or polyunsaturated. It's not the total amount of fat in a diet that is linked to heart disease, cancer and other life-threatening or debilitating conditions — it's the type and balance of fat.

TRANS FATS

Trans fats, which have become the centre of attention recently, are 'bad fats'. They are formed through a process called hydrogenation which turns vegetable and animal liquid oils into solid fats.

Small amounts of trans fats can occur naturally in some meat and dairy products, but the largest source of trans fats is in processed foods: doughnuts, biscuits, cookies, cakes, icing, pastries, deep-fat fried foods (including those from all major 'fast-food' chains), potato crisps and corn snacks, imitation cheeses, and confectionery where the fats are used to extend shelf life.

Trans fats reduce 'good cholesterol' (HDL — high-density lipoprotein) and increase 'bad cholesterol' (LDL — low-density lipoprotein), contributing to the build-up of fatty plaque; a thick, hard deposit that can narrow the arteries and make them less flexible. If a clot forms in a narrowed artery, it can result in a heart attack or stroke. Low levels of HDL also increase the risk of heart disease. So trans fats, by definition, are bad for your heart.

High levels of HDL cholesterol, on the other hand, seem to protect against heart attacks. Some experts believe that HDL removes excess cholesterol from arterial plaque, thus slowing its build-up. Medical experts think that HDL tends to carry cholesterol away from the arteries and back to the liver, where it is passed from the body.

NORMAL ARTERY VERSUS BLOCKED ARTERY

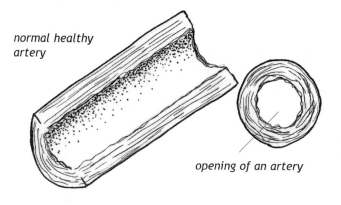

normal healthy artery

opening of an artery

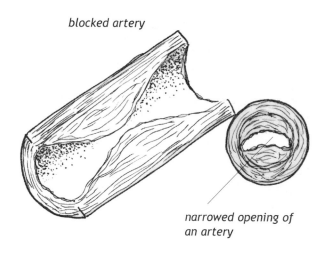

blocked artery

narrowed opening of an artery

Most people in the UK eat less than the limit recommended for trans fats, but since they haven't got any nutritional value, many retailers have pledged to reduce them or completely remove them in the near future. This is not the case for saturated fats.

SATURATED FATS

Most of us continue to consume far greater levels of saturated fats than is healthy for us. Saturated fat is a fat that is solid at room temperature and comes chiefly from animal food products. Some examples are butter, lard, meat dripping and goose fat. In addition to animal fats, there are three tropical oils that we have been told should be avoided because they tend to raise cholesterol levels: these are coconut, palm and palm kernel oils.

MONO- AND POLYUNSATURATED FATS

Unsaturated fats are fats found in products derived from plant sources. Polyunsaturated fats tend to lower blood cholesterol. Monounsaturated fats boast an added bonus — they maintain HDL. But even though polyunsaturated and monounsaturated fats are considered more desirable choices, they, too, should be limited to no more than 10% of total calorie intake.

Monounsaturated fats are liquid at room temperature, but cloud and thicken when chilled. Consuming monounsaturated fats seems to reduce total blood cholesterol and the 'bad' low-density lipoprotein (LDL) cholesterol levels without affecting the 'good' high-density lipoprotein (HDL) cholesterol levels.

Polyunsaturated fats remain liquid whether they are at room temperature or in the refrigerator. Polyunsaturated fats used to be the healthy heroes because they reduce total cholesterol and LDL, but we now know they also decrease HDL's positive effects. However, it is some polyunsaturated oils that contain the omegas.

SWINGS AND ROUNDABOUTS

To further confuse the 'good fats vs. bad fats' issue, there are now some health practitioners who believe that some of the fats previously thought of as 'unhealthy' actually offer health benefits.

COCONUT OIL

Coconut oil is currently being touted as a 'healthy' oil by some despite its high level of saturated fat. Those who are advocating it claim that it contains lauric acid, found in mother's milk. It is an unprocessed culinary oil with a delicious aroma and flavour, it helps maintain healthy HDL and LDL ratios, it supports healthy thyroid function and contains antibacterial, antiviral and antifungal properties.

PALM OIL
The benefits of palm oil supposedly are that it contains no 'bad' trans fats, and is cholesterol- and GM-free. It also purports to be a good source of beta-carotene. Palm oil is said to be an excellent dietary energy source and has a high vitamin A and E content.

However, the fact remains that both coconut oil and palm oil are high in saturated fat and therefore may lead to cardiovascular disease.

OMEGA-3, 6 AND 9
And last, but not least, there is omega. Omega is the last letter of the Greek alphabet. In nutritional healthy fat terms, 'the omegas' are probably the most studied. This family of essential fatty acids (EFAs) includes omega-3, omega-6 and omega-9. These EFAs provide support for numerous bodily functions, including the cardiovascular, reproductive, immune and nervous systems. Both omega-3 (found in flaxseed and hemp seed oils, oily fish, walnuts and pumpkin seeds) and omega-6 (found in safflower, sunflower, corn, sesame, hemp seed, pumpkin, soybean, walnut and wheatgerm) contain the EFAs your body needs but can't produce on its own. For that reason they must be taken through food or supplementation.

Omega-9, while not considered essential, also provides substantial health benefits and should be part of a good dietary lifestyle because of its monounsaturated oleic acid content. This plays a protective role in reducing heart attack risk, preventing arterial cholesterol build-up and is also believed to assist in cancer prevention. Olive oil, avocados and various nuts (peanuts, almonds and macadamia nuts) are rich omega-9 sources.

It seems to be the balance of omegas that is important. Today, most experts believe that we get too much omega-

6 through many of our cooking oils and processed foods and too little omega-3 from oily fish, fish oil supplements and plant oils. It is important to take these fatty acids in the proper ratio. The ratio of omega-6 to omega-3 should be about 2:1. In the Western world, the real ratio is somewhere in between 10:1 to 20:1.

But before we all rush out to buy omega-3 supplements in tablet form, we should think about changing our diets. It is suggested that healthy adults should consume at least two servings of oily fish per week to restore the omega balance. Vegetarians should concentrate on flaxseeds and oil and hemp seed oil. One teaspoon (5ml) of oil or one tablespoon (15ml) of seed will supply the daily requirement.

Omega-3 fatty acids are found in oily fish like salmon and flaxseed and canola oils.

Another consideration is that it is possible to overdose on omega-3. Heart patients, hoping to increase their chances, might be overzealous in their ingestion of omega-3; eating lots of oily fish, and good oils, following a Mediterranean-style diet plus taking supplements. This could cause excessive bleeding and other problems. Fish oil supplements can also adversely react with certain medications, such as warfarin, aspirin and clopidogrel and should only be taken after discussion with your doctor.

How to Buy and Store Oils

HOW TO BUY AND STORE OILS

Many culinary oils are sold in gourmet, ethnic, speciality food shops or on the internet. Some of the more familiar and 'trendy' oils are also available from supermarkets.

The single most important factor in buying any cooking oil is quality. If you have a choice, select cold- or expeller-pressed oils to ensure maximum purity, flavour and nutrition.

Oil, unlike wine, does not improve with age. Buying oil in small sizes, or splitting larger bottles with friends, is a practical way to buy expensive oils. Oil purchased in bulk should always be poured into smaller containers. (A large bottle of oil at a good price is no bargain if you end up throwing most of it away.) Tinted glass, porcelain or stainless steel are the best materials for containers; oil should never be stored in plastic or in reactive metals. Stay away from plastic containers as the oil can absorb PVCs (polyvinyl chlorides). Various toxic chemicals are added to plastic containers as 'plasticisers'. Traces of these chemicals, known as adipates and phthalates, can leak out of PVC into foods.

To store expensive extra virgin olive oil, a kitchen cupboard located away from the oven and hob and not next to direct sunlight will work quite well. It is best to store most other oils in the refrigerator or in a cool, dry place. For more precise information, read the label. Oils may thicken, turn cloudy and even solidify, perhaps, but if you let them stand at room temperature, they will soon return to their liquid state. Refined oils high in monounsaturated fats will keep up to a year, while those high in polyunsaturated fats will keep about six months.

Air, heat and light will cause oils to turn rancid. Rancid oil has an unpleasant aroma and acrid taste and its nutrient value is greatly diminished. Discard rancid oils immediately since they are the worst kinds of fat you can consume.

Heating oils beyond their smoke point is also undesirable. The longer an oil is heated, the more quickly it will decompose. Avoid preheating the oil any longer than necessary. If you're cooking more than one batch of food, quickly add each new batch unless time is needed to adjust the temperature. Turn off the heat as soon as you have removed the last batch of food.

Cool used oil in its pan. If you will be using it again, pour it through a sieve and funnel into a clean bottle. Never pour hot used oil back into the bottle with the unused oil. Always discard oil that has reached its smoke point, along with any food that has been in contact with it. Never pour hot oil down the drain. If you will not be using that batch of oil again, wait until it is cool, pour into an appropriate container and discard.

Health Benefits of Culinary Oils

HEALTH BENEFITS OF CULINARY OILS

What is becoming crystal clear is that 'bad' fats, i.e., saturated and trans fats, increase the risk for certain diseases while 'good' fats, meaning monounsaturated and polyunsaturated fats, reduce the risk. The key is to substitute good fats for bad fats.

What about cholesterol? Although it is still important to limit the amount of cholesterol you produce, especially if you have diabetes, dietary cholesterol isn't nearly the villain it's been portrayed to be. Cholesterol in the bloodstream is what's most important. High blood cholesterol levels greatly increase the risk of heart disease. But the average person makes about 75% of blood cholesterol in his or her liver, while only about 25% is absorbed from food. The biggest influence on blood cholesterol level is the mix of fats in the diet.

BLOOD CHOLESTEROL

The Cholesterol-Heart Disease Connection
Cholesterol is a waxy substance that the liver makes and links to carrier proteins called lipoproteins that let it dissolve in blood and be transported to all parts of the body.

Too much cholesterol in the blood, though, can lead to problems. In the 1960s and 70s, scientists established a link between high blood cholesterol levels and heart disease. Deposits of cholesterol can build up inside arteries. These deposits, called plaque, can narrow an artery enough to slow or block blood flow. This narrowing process, called atherosclerosis, commonly occurs in arteries that nourish the heart (coronary arteries). When one or more sections of heart muscle fail to get enough blood and the oxygen and nutrients they need, the result may be a chest pain known as angina. In addition, plaque can rupture, causing blood clots that may lead to heart attack, stroke, or sudden death. Fortunately, the build-up of cholesterol can be slowed, stopped or even reversed.

Cholesterol-carrying lipoproteins play central roles in the development of atherosclerotic plaque and cardiovascular disease. The two main types of lipoproteins basically work in opposite directions.

Low-density lipoproteins (LDL) carry cholesterol from the liver to the rest of the body. When there is too much LDL cholesterol in the blood, it can be deposited on the walls of the coronary arteries. Because of this, LDL cholesterol is often referred to as the 'bad' cholesterol.

High-density lipoproteins (HDL) carry cholesterol from the blood back to the liver, which processes the cholesterol for elimination from the body. HDL makes it less likely that excess cholesterol in the blood will be deposited in the coronary arteries, which is why HDL cholesterol is often referred to as the 'good' cholesterol.

In general, the higher your LDL and the lower your HDL, the greater your risk for atherosclerosis and heart disease.

Doctors keep reducing the tolerance of cholesterol-carrying lipoproteins they think we should maintain, even as they prevaricate about the numbers of HDL and LDL. The general level of acceptance among British cardiologists these days seems to be a total HDL + LDL of no more than 4.0; some are even advocating 3.0.

Some experts believe that taking fish oil in any form can help regulate cholesterol in the body, because fish oil has high levels of omega-3. Aside from cholesterol regulation, benefits include anti-inflammatory properties and positive effects on body composition.

The bottom line is the recommendation to increase consumption of oils that are high in omega-3: olive oil, rapeseed oil, hemp seed oil and flaxseed oil.

HEART DISEASE AND HIGH BLOOD PRESSURE

Flaxseed has a whole menu of ailments it supposedly prevents or helps.

It helps protect the body against high blood pressure, inflammation, water retention, sticky platelets which can cause blood clots and lowered immune function.

Pine nut oil also claims cardiovascular benefits: scientists have demonstrated that pinolenic acid favourably affects total blood lipids, reduces platelet aggregation and lowers blood pressure, contributing to cardiovascular health.

DIETARY FATS AND CANCER

Heart disease is not the only condition that has been linked with fat intake. Researchers suspected an association between dietary fat and certain cancers. Here again, the type of fat — and not the total amount — seemed to be most important.

Breast Cancer

By the early 1980s, most nutrition experts believed that dietary fat was a major cause of breast cancer. This thinking was largely based on international comparisons showing higher breast cancer rates in countries with higher per capita fat intake. But such comparisons are very broad in nature. As more detailed studies were performed over the next couple of decades, the apparent link between total fat intake and breast cancer has faded. The Women's Health Initiative Dietary Modification Trial (WHIDMT), which was specifically designed to examine the effect of a low-fat diet on the development of breast cancer, showed similar rates of breast cancer in women eating a low-fat diet and in those eating a 'regular' diet.

Other studies — including those by Harvard researchers — of different types of fat have failed to find a link with breast cancer. However, some European studies have reported findings of lower breast cancer risk among women with a high intake of monounsaturated fats (mainly in the form of olive oil).

Those who ate the most fat had an 11% higher incidence of breast cancer than those who ate the least. The increase in risk was similar whether the women were eating saturated, monounsaturated or polyunsaturated fats. Taking into account family history of breast cancer, smoking, body mass index and alcohol intake did not affect the results.

However, those women with the highest fat intake were more likely to have been taking hormone replacement therapy (HRT) which has been linked to breast cancer when they joined the study. This suggests that fat may affect breast cancer risk by stimulating hormone production.

Colon Cancer

As with breast cancer, international comparisons initially suggested an association between total dietary fat intake and colon cancer risk. But later studies contradicted these earlier findings and revealed instead an association that was weak at best. As was the case with breast cancer, women in the WHIDMT who ate a low-fat diet developed colon cancer at the same rate as women who didn't. Although fat intake doesn't seem to increase colon cancer risk, high consumption of red meat still does appear to do so.

Prostate Cancer

Although the exact connection between dietary fat and prostate cancer is far from clear, there is some evidence that diets high in animal fat and saturated fat increase prostate cancer risk. However, some studies have also shown no association, while others have implicated unsaturated fats. Clearly, much more research is needed to clear up the exact links between dietary fat and prostate cancer.

Other Cancers

Preliminary research has also linked the intake of certain kinds of fat with other cancers, though much more research is needed to confirm these results. In the Nurses' Health Study, Harvard researchers found that a high intake of trans fats increased the risk for non-

Hodgkin's lymphoma and that a high saturated fat intake increased the risk for endometrial cancer.

In conclusion, many studies about fatty acids and cancer are contradictory. One study says that omega-3 fatty acids inhibit cancer growth. Another says that these fatty acids increase cancer growth! The bottom line is that more research must be done.

DIETARY FATS AND OBESITY

It is a common belief that the more fat you eat, the more body fat you put on, and the more weight you gain. This belief has been bolstered by much of the nutrition advice given to people over the past decade, which has focused on lowering total fat intake while increasing carbohydrate intake. But it isn't completely true, and the advice has been misguided. For example, while Americans have gradually decreased the proportion of calories they get from fat over the last decade, rates of obesity have increased steeply.

Over the short term, following a low-fat diet does lead to weight loss. But so does following a high-fat, low-carbohydrate diet. Actually, almost any diet that helps you take in fewer calories works over the short term. In other words, low-fat diets appear to offer no apparent advantages over diets with fat levels close to the national average. This was demonstrated in the WHIDMT. Women in this trial who were assigned to a low-fat diet did not lose, or gain, any more weight than women eating a 'usual' diet.

Although more research is needed, a prudent recommendation for losing weight or maintaining a healthy weight is to be mindful of the amount of food you eat in relation to the amount of calories you burn in a day. Exercising regularly is essential.

Because of the continuing obesity epidemic, one of the lesser-known oils became the subject of close scrutiny by nutritionists and researchers as a natural way to promote 'fullness' and curb overeating.

According to a study by Lipid Nutrition, the pinolenic acid contained in pine nut oil can help curb appetite by stimulating the release of a hormone that functions as an appetite suppressant. The study showed that pine nut oil 'boosts appetite suppressors up to 60% for four hours'. This was already understood in Siberia where a handful of pine nuts or a tablespoonful of pine nut oil has traditionally been taken with (or instead of) a meal when food is scarce.

RECOMMENDATIONS FOR HEALTHY FAT INTAKE
Although the different types of fat have a varied and admittedly confusing effect on health and disease, the basic message is simple: chuck out the bad fats and replace them with good fats.

Body Care and Alternative Therapies

BODY CARE AND ALTERNATIVE THERAPIES

Who knew cooking oil could do so much else?!
There are a lot of nefarious claims made by skin care
brands saying their products make skin smoother,
hydrated, younger-looking and so forth. Many of the oils
we have previously discussed do benefit the skin in some
way or another and there are several oils that appear to
offer actual health benefits. Since I can't prove that they
will work as advertised, I offer a caution. It is essential
that any time you put a new product on your skin, no
matter how natural, you should always do a patch test to
ensure you are not allergic to it.

Almond Oil is an excellent emollient (softening and
soothing to the skin). It is also an effective moisturiser
suitable for all skin types, helping to relieve irritation,
inflammation and itching. It is a good lubricant and
because it is not a very fast penetrating oil, it is an
excellent massage oil because it can be spread all over
the body while still allowing you time to do a good
massage before it is absorbed by the skin. It can also help
to relieve muscular aches and pains. Although mostly
used on its own as a massage carrier oil, it also works
well by diluting with 10% wheatgerm oil to help give it a
longer shelf life. Almond oil is one of the most popular
carrier oils since it is non-greasy, spreads easily and also
is great for nourishing the skin.

Apricot kernel oil also makes significant skin care claims.
It's rich in vitamin E, which helps the skin maintain
elasticity, suppleness and clarity as it ages. Since apricot
kernel oil easily penetrates the skin without leaving an
oily residue, it is good oil for sensitive, prematurely aged,
dry or irritated skin. Apricot kernel oil is also popular as a
massage oil and is used as a carrier oil for essential oils in
aromatherapy.

Fish oil Generic fish oil is defined as oil derived from oily
fish. It can come from the liver or other organs or fish
flesh. Some experts believe that taking fish oil in any
form, whether by eating the fish or taking the oil as a
nutritional supplement, can help regulate cholesterol in

the body because fish oil has high levels of omega-3 fatty acids. In addition, benefits include anti-inflammatory properties and other advantages to the body.

The most common fish oil is cod liver oil, derived from cod livers. It is a nutritional supplement; in the past most commonly given to children. Cod liver oil is one of the most effective providers of omega-3 and an excellent source of vitamins A and D. In adults, it is usually taken to ease the pain and joint stiffness associated with arthritis as well as helping to nourish skin, hair and nails.

Grapeseed oil is one of the most common oils used for massage. It is good for those people whose skin does not seem to absorb oil easily. When it is used in skin care products, it is usually blended with other more nutrient-rich carriers. It is ideal for use in products for thin, greasy, damaged and delicate hair, lip balms, hand creams and regenerative products for mature, damaged and stressed skin, notably for use around the eyes and neck.

Hazelnut oil is well-known for its astringent qualities. It is deeply penetrating and stimulating to the circulatory system and is high in vitamins, minerals and protein. Its texture makes it an excellent moisturiser for those with oily skin, suitable particularly for facial and body massages giving a smooth, silky-soft skin texture and is a lovely carrier oil.

Hemp seed oil naturally replenishes skin moisture. If you suffer from eczema, psoriasis, skin cracking or scaling, chapped lips or dry hair, systematic use of skin care products containing omega-6 fatty acids should restore your skin's natural glow and bring a healthy sheen to your hair and lips. Because hemp seed oil is an excellent source of omega fatty acids, adding it to your diet can substantially improve your skin's natural appearance and elasticity.

Macadamia nut oil is one of the best regenerative oils available. It closely resembles sebum (the oil naturally produced by the skin to help protect it). Macadamia oil is a fabulous, protective oil with a high absorption rate and has been successfully used as a healing oil for scars, sunburn, minor wounds and other irritations.

Olive oil has been used by Mediterranean people for centuries to help maintain good health, a fresh, dewy complexion, lustrous hair, and more. It is probably the most universally popular oil, prized for a multitude of uses. Among other things, olive oil can be used as a soak for brittle and dry fingernails and ragged cuticles. It smooths and softens hands and feet and relieves chapped lips. For lustrous hair, massage a few tablespoonfuls of olive oil into the hair, cover it with a shower cap and leave on for 30 minutes or more, then shampoo as usual. To get rid of frizz, put a small drop of olive oil into your palm, rub your hands together and apply to dry hair. Adding several tablespoonfuls to the bath, along with your favourite essential oil, will soothe and nourish the skin.

Olive oil soap bars

Pecan nut oil is sold as a pleasant, lightweight massage oil with the ability to soothe and soften dry skin. Some companies incorporate the oil into soap bars.

Pistachio nut oil also has some cosmetic interest. Excellent for the skin, pistachio nut oil nourishes, softens and hydrates the skin thanks to the vitamins it contains. Used in massage, it is easily absorbed by the skin and gives it a supple and soft texture.

Sesame seed oil is immensely popular in India where its use is part of everyday life and an important aspect of Ayurveda massage, ancient Indian techniques that provide relaxation, improved circulation and elimination of toxins. Sesame is the favoured massage oil as its chemical structure gives it a unique ability to penetrate the skin easily, nourishing and detoxifying even the deepest tissue layers.

It is naturally antibacterial, antiviral and an anti-inflammatory agent. It has been successfully used in the hair of children to kill lice infestations and used after exposure to wind or sun to calm sunburn. It nourishes and feeds the scalp to control dry scalp dandruff and to kill dandruff-causing bacteria. It protects the skin from the effects of chlorine in swimming pool water. It is also good for facial application in controlling acne.

Safflower and **Sunflower oils** can help to moisturise, regenerate, soften and condition the skin. Two of the most popular carrier oils, they are suitable for sensitive, dry or damaged skin.

Tea tree oil displays a number of remarkable properties making it very effective for a wide range of complaints. Foremost and what makes tea tree outstanding in comparison to other remedies is that it is active against all three varieties of infectious organisms: bacteria, fungi and viruses. It has been proved effective in the treatment of acne, athlete's foot, blisters, burns, cold sores, dandruff, herpes, insect bites, oily skin, general skin rashes and nappy rash. The antiseptic and bacterial properties of tea tree oil aid in the treatment of cuts, burns, insect bites, infected splinters and all kinds of wounds, especially dirty wounds or those which contain pus. Because of its antifungal properties, tea tree is an effective treatment for ringworm, athlete's foot and thrush (*candida*).

Viruses are the invading organisms responsible for most epidemic illnesses. As a powerful antiviral agent, it is *claimed* that tea tree is effective in fighting many common infectious diseases such as measles, chicken pox, flu, cold and shingles, as well as other viral complaints, i.e., cold sores, verrucae and warts.

It is also said that tea tree is of great value as a preventative remedy to help the body fight off all kinds of infection. This is especially important if the body is already in a weakened condition brought on by stress, illness or the use of antibiotics or other drugs which have lowered the body's natural resistance levels. It can be helpful to those who need to build up their strength before a surgical operation or for those suffering from chronic or long-standing debilitating illness.

Tea tree oil really seems to be the wonder oil! It can be topically applied to the skin, used in the bath, or for inhalation in a vaporiser. **It should not be taken internally.**

Wheatgerm oil is ultra-rich and can be a useful addition to massage and aromatherapy oils, especially for rough skin areas. Try mixing wheatgerm with other lighter carrier oils, such as almond oil, as wheat germ may be too sticky when used on its own.

Recipes

STARTERS AND SIDE DISHES

ASPARAGUS ROASTED WITH HAZELNUT OIL

Serves 4–6

> 900 g (2 lb) fresh asparagus, tough ends snapped off
> Sea salt to taste
> Freshly ground black pepper to taste
> 30 ml (2 tbsp) hazelnut oil*

1 Preheat the oven to 190°C (375°F/gas mark 5).

2 Peel the lower third of the asparagus stalks, unless they are very young and tender.

3 Place the asparagus in one layer in a baking dish, season with salt and pepper and drizzle with half the hazelnut oil.

4 Roast for 12-14 minutes, depending on the size of the asparagus.

5 Remove from the oven and drizzle with the remainder of the hazelnut oil. Serve immediately.

* Extra virgin olive oil, walnut oil or avocado oil may be substituted, if preferred.

BOURBON CHICKEN WINGS

Serves 4–6

> 24 chicken wings, tips cut off and reserved for stock
> 45 ml (3 tbsp) bourbon whiskey
> 45 ml (3 tbsp) olive oil
> 15 ml (1 tbsp) grated lemon rind
> Juice of 1 lemon
> 115 g (4 oz) unseasoned breadcrumbs
> 15 ml (1 tbsp) Hungarian paprika
> Sea salt and freshly ground black pepper to taste

1 Combine the chicken wings, bourbon whiskey, olive oil, lemon rind and lemon juice in a bowl. Toss to coat the wings and marinate in the refrigerator for 4 hours or overnight.

2 Preheat the grill to high.

3 Mix the breadcrumbs, paprika, salt and pepper in a plastic bag. Drain the chicken wings and toss with the breadcrumb mixture. Place the wings on a baking sheet about 12 cm (5 in) from the heat. Grill until crisp and golden, about 5 minutes on each side.

BRUSCHETTA

Serves 6

Bruschetta is one of the simplest things in the world to make, and can be very satisfying if you have good extra virgin olive oil.

6 slices x 15 cm (6 in) wide fresh crusty Italian bread
Garlic clove
Extra virgin olive oil
Sea salt and freshly ground black pepper
Chopped fresh ripe tomatoes
Fresh basil, chopped

1 Toast the bread, gently rub with a cut clove of garlic and drizzle with a good, fruity olive oil.

2 Season with salt and pepper to taste, cut the bread slices in half and spread with a layer of chopped tomatoes. Grind some pepper over the tomatoes, sprinkle with basil and drizzle a little more olive oil over all.

CHEESE AND BACON POTATO ROUNDS

Serves 4

4 baking potatoes, sliced 1 cm (½ in) thick
60 ml (4 tbsp) avocado oil
8 slices streaky bacon, cooked and crumbled
115 g (4 oz) Cheddar cheese, grated
3-4 spring onions, chopped

1 Preheat the oven to 200°C (400°F/gas mark 6).

2 Brush both sides of the potato slices with avocado oil and place them on an ungreased baking sheet. Bake in the oven for 30 minutes or so, turning halfway through, or until lightly browned on both sides.

3 Remove from the oven and top with the bacon, cheese and spring onions.

4 Return to the oven and continue baking until the cheese melts. Serve hot.

CHINESE ROASTED NUTS

Makes about 340 g (12 oz)

> 115 g (4 oz) unsalted cashew nuts
> 115 g (4 oz) unsalted peanuts
> 115 g (4 oz) sunflower seeds
> 15 ml (1 tbsp) sesame oil
> 15 ml (1 tbsp) soy sauce
> 5 ml (1 tsp) dark brown sugar
> 2.5 ml (½ tsp) Chinese five-spice powder

1 Preheat the oven to 180°C (350°F/gas mark 4).

2 Combine all ingredients in a bowl and toss to thoroughly coat the nuts.

3 Spread on a baking sheet and roast until lightly toasted, about 15 minutes.

4 Cool and store in an airtight container. Serve as a snack or with drinks.

GRILLED PORTOBELLO MUSHROOMS AND GOAT'S CHEESE

Serves 4

225 g (8 oz) mild goat's cheese, sliced
4 large Portobello mushrooms

Sauce:

60 ml (4 tbsp) garlic-infused olive oil
Sea salt and freshly ground black pepper
75 ml (5 tbsp) chopped fresh raw baby spinach
60 ml (4 tbsp) chopped fresh basil
5 ml (1 tsp) fresh thyme leaves
15 ml (1 tbsp) balsamic vinegar
5 ml (1 tsp) capers (optional)
2 cloves roasted garlic
Pine nuts or pine nut oil (optional)

Salad or risotto to serve

1 Preheat the grill to high.

2 In a blender or food processor, blend all the sauce ingredients together.

3 Line the grill pan with aluminium foil and place the mushrooms on it, underside down. Brush with sauce and grill for 4–5 minutes. Turn the mushrooms cap-side up and grill for an additional 3–4 minutes. Turn the mushrooms again, add the goat's cheese and any additional sauce and grill until the cheese melts.

4 Serve with a simple salad or risotto.

COCONUT PRAWNS WITH MARMALADE SAUCE

Serves 6

For the prawns:

    55 g (2 oz) plain flour

    30 g (1 oz) cornflour

    5 ml (1 tsp) Jamaican jerk seasoning

    240 ml (8 fl oz) unsweetened coconut milk

    115 g (4 oz) shredded wheat cereal, crushed

    Rapeseed or sunflower oil for frying

    45 g (1½ oz) flaked coconut

    24 large headless raw prawns, shelled, but with tail shell
        attached (about 675 g/1½ lb)

For the dipping sauce:

    450 g (1 lb) orange marmalade

    15 ml (1 tbsp) lime juice

    10 ml (2 tsp) rapeseed oil

    1.25 ml (¼ tsp) sea salt

    2.5 ml (½ tsp) freshly ground black pepper

    1.25 ml (¼ tsp) hot pepper sauce (or to taste)

1 Pour 5 cm (2 in) oil into a deep frying pan or wok and heat to 180°C (350°F).

2 In a shallow bowl, combine flour, cornflour and jerk seasoning. Pour coconut milk into a second bowl. In a third bowl or shallow plate, combine the crushed shredded wheat and flaked coconut. Lay out wire racks and place parchment paper underneath them to catch drippings.

3 Make the dipping sauce. Place all ingredients into a food processor and pulse until almost smooth.

4 Hold each prawn by the tail, coat with the flour mixture, dip into the coconut milk and coat with the crushed wheat/coconut mixture. Place prawns on the wire racks and repeat process until all prawns are coated.

5 Carefully lower the prawns into the oil, frying about six at a time, for 2 minutes or until golden and crisp. Bring oil back to temperature before frying next batch. As each batch finishes, drain prawns on a paper towel before transferring to a serving platter. Serve hot or warm with dip.

ROASTED GARLIC AND OLIVES

Serves 4

2–4 heads fresh garlic bulbs
60 ml (4 tbsp) virgin olive oil
Good handful of assorted olives
Crusty bread to serve

1 Preheat the oven to 200°C (400°F/gas mark 6).

2 Peel away the outer layers of the garlic bulb skin, leaving the skin of the individual cloves intact. Using a knife, cut off about 1 cm (¼-½ in) from the top of the garlic, exposing the individual cloves.

3 Place the garlic, cut-side up, in a small roasting or pie tin and drizzle with the olive oil. Cover tightly with aluminium foil. Roast for 30–35 minutes, or until the garlic is soft when gently squeezed. Cool slightly, then set out on a platter with the olives and bread. To eat, squeeze the garlic from its skin onto crusty bread, accompanied by the olives.

SPICED POTATO CAKES WITH CORIANDER AND MINT CHUTNEY

Serves 4

450 g (1 lb) potatoes
30 ml (2 tbsp) rapeseed oil
1 large onion, thinly sliced
15 ml (1 tbsp) cumin seeds
5 ml (1 tsp) salt
15 ml (1 tbsp) garam masala
1-2 fresh green chillies, finely chopped

Coriander and mint chutney:
Handful of fresh coriander leaves
Handful of fresh mint leaves
1 fresh green chilli (optional)
15ml (1 tbsp) lemon juice
200 g (7 oz) plain yogurt
Pinch of sea salt

1 Place the potatoes in a pan of salted water, bring to the boil and cook until soft. Drain.

2 Roughly chop the potatoes into a large mixing bowl.

3 Heat 15ml (1 tbsp) of the rapeseed oil in a frying pan and fry the onion for 30 seconds. Add the cumin seeds. Continue to cook until the onions are soft and translucent.

4 Tip the onions into the bowl containing the potatoes, along with the salt, garam masala and chillies. Wipe the frying pan with a paper towel and set aside.

5 Mash the ingredients with a fork to combine. Cool in the refrigerator for about 30 minutes.

6 To make the chutney, put the coriander, mint, chilli if using, lemon juice and 45 ml (3 tbsp) water in the container of a blender or food processor. Blend until smooth, pushing down if necessary with a rubber spatula. Whisk the yogurt in a small bowl until creamy.

Add the coriander mixture and fold in. Add the salt. Chill until needed.

7 Divide the potato mixture into 12 equal portions. Take a portion and roll into a ball, then flatten to make an even disc. Repeat with the remaining portions and place on a plate.

8 Heat the remaining oil in the clean frying pan until hot and fry the cakes in batches for a few minutes on each side until golden-brown. Serve hot or at room temperature with coriander and mint chutney.

VEGETARIAN SPRING ROLLS

Bring some Asian flair to your table with these easy-to-prepare spring rolls. The colourful cabbage and pepper filling is tangy and delicious. They can be prepared several hours ahead and fried right before serving. And feel free to experiment with different flavours and ingredients in the dipping sauce.

Serves 4–6

    1 pack (20 sheets) spring roll wrappers
    2 red peppers
    2 yellow peppers
    2 green peppers
    1 small white cabbage
    60 ml (4 tbsp) tamari soy sauce
    5 ml (1 tsp) fresh chopped ginger or 2.5ml
       (½ tsp) ground ginger
    3 sprigs fresh coriander
    Freshly ground black pepper to taste

Dipping sauce:

    120 ml (4 fl oz) tamari soy sauce
    60 ml (4 tbsp) rice wine vinegar or white wine vinegar

    Oil for frying, such as sesame seed oil
    Salad garnish to serve

1 Cut the peppers and cabbage into julienne strips.

2 Add the first lot of soy sauce, minced ginger and coriander to the mixture and season with freshly ground black pepper.

3 Place a small quantity of the filling in the centre of a spring roll wrapper and wrap tightly, tucking in the ends.

4 Chill in the refrigerator until needed.

5 Make the dipping sauce by mixing the remaining
   120 ml (4 fl oz) tamari soy sauce and the vinegar
   together in a small bowl.

6 Heat enough sesame oil in a wok or frying pan for
   shallow frying and fry until golden and crisp. Serve
   immediately with the dipping sauce and salad garnish.

BAKED ONIONS

Serves 4–6

   4-6 large sweet onions
   30-45 ml (2-3 tbsp) avocado oil
   10-15 ml (2-3 tsp) caraway seeds
   Sea salt and freshly ground black pepper to taste

1 Preheat the oven to 180°C (350°F/gas mark 4).

2 Peel the onions and, using the tip of a small knife, cut
   a small hole, about 2.5 cm (1 in) deep in the root end.
   Brush the onions with some of the oil, then spoon the
   remainder into the depressions. Sprinkle with the
   caraway seeds and season with salt and pepper.

3 Place the onions in a suitable baking dish and bake for
   1 hour, until the onions are soft and melting.

FRIED GREEN TOMATOES

Serves 4–6

    115 g (4 oz) self-raising flour
    115 g (4 oz) finely ground maize meal
    5 ml (1 tsp) garlic powder
    5 ml (1 tsp) coarse-ground black pepper
    1.25 ml (¼ tsp) cayenne pepper
    240 ml (8 fl oz) buttermilk, or milk soured
        with 15 ml (1 tbsp) lemon juice or vinegar
    1 medium egg
    4-8 green tomatoes, the greener the better, depending on
        size
    Sunflower or safflower oil to shallow-fry

1 Slice the green tomatoes, about 1 cm (½ in) thick.

2 Combine the flour, maize meal and seasonings in a
   shallow dish. Whisk the egg and buttermilk together in
   another dish.

3 Dip tomato slices in flour mix, then in buttermilk mix,
   then in flour mix again. You can prepare all the
   tomato slices at once, placing them on a baking
   sheet.

4 Heat the oil in a large frying pan and working in
   batches, fry the coated tomato slices in hot vegetable
   oil until just browned on each side. Keep warm.

THYME AND BLACK PEPPER
HASSLEBACK POTATOES

Serves 4–6

   12 small roasting potatoes (about 900 g/2 lb)
   30 ml (2 tbsp) sunflower oil
   30 ml (2 tbsp) olive oil
   10 ml (2 tsp) coarse-ground black pepper
   5 ml (1 tsp) dried thyme
   Sea salt to taste
   Fresh thyme sprigs to garnish

1 Preheat the oven to 200°C (400°F/gas mark 6).

2 Peel the potatoes and cut in half lengthways so they
   lie flat.

3 Slice each potato vertically three-quarters of the way
   through at 5 mm (¼ in) intervals, keeping them joined
   at the base. Wipe the potatoes dry with a paper towel.

4 Pour the sunflower and olive oils into a baking pan,
   add the thyme, salt and pepper and toss the potatoes
   in the oil mixture. Arrange cut-side down in the pan.

5 Roast in the centre of the oven for 30 minutes; turn
   the potatoes cut-side up and roast for a further 20–30
   minutes, until golden and crisp.

6 Serve garnished with fresh thyme sprigs.

SALADS, SALAD DRESSINGS AND SOUPS

AUTUMN SALAD WITH BLUE CHEESE

Serves 6

> 400 g (14 oz) mixed salad leaves, torn into manageable
>   pieces
> 1 medium eating apple, diced
> 30 g (1 oz) crumbled mild blue cheese
> 30 g (1 oz) toasted pecans, chopped for garnish

For the dressing:
> 60 ml (4 tbsp) orange juice
> 60 ml (4 tbsp) rapeseed oil
> 45 ml (3 tbsp) cider vinegar
> 5 ml (1 tsp) sugar
> 1.25 ml (¼ tsp) sea salt
> Freshly ground black pepper

1 Combine the dressing ingredients in a screw-topped
   jar. Shake to combine and chill in the refrigerator to
   blend the flavours.

2 Tip the salad leaves, apple and blue cheese into a
   bowl and toss with the dressing. Serve, garnished with
   the toasted pecans.

BROAD BEAN SALAD

Serves 4-6

450 g (1 lb) fresh or frozen young broad breans
1 red onion, chopped
3 medium-size ripe tomatoes, chopped
1 rib celery, strings removed and chopped
15 g (½ oz) fresh curly parsley, chopped
60 ml (2 fl oz) extra virgin olive oil
45 ml (3 tbsp) red wine vinegar
15 ml (1 tbsp) fresh chopped thyme leaves
Pinch of sea salt
1 clove garlic, finely chopped

1 Cook the broad beans until tender, drain and cool.

2 In a large bowl, mix the broad beans with all the remaining ingredients. Cover and refrigerate until needed, bringing it up to cool room temperature before serving.

CANELLINI BEAN AND CHERRY TOMATO SALAD

Serves 6-8

This salad combines the sweetness of cherry tomatoes with buttery canellini beans and parsley. The secret is in the dressing, which includes garlic and rosemary-infused olive oil, and a paste made of garlic, lemon, Parmesan cheese and anchovies. Omit the anchovies for a vegetarian option.

420 g (15 oz) tin canellini beans, drained and rinsed
250 g (9 oz) cherry tomatoes, halved
Handful coarsely chopped parsley

For the dressing:

60 ml (4 tbsp) extra virgin olive oil
3 cloves garlic, peeled and crushed
7.5 cm (3 in) sprig of fresh rosemary
3 anchovy fillets, coarsely chopped (optional)
30 g (1 oz) freshly-grated Parmesan cheese
4 ml (¾ tsp) sea salt
1.25 ml (¼ tsp) freshly ground black pepper
5 ml (1 tsp) grated lemon rind
60 ml (4 tbsp) lemon juice

1 Make the dressing. Put the olive oil, garlic and rosemary in a small saucepan over a medium heat until the rosemary begins to sizzle. Remove the pan from the heat and let stand for 20 minutes, allowing the rosemary and garlic to infuse in the oil.

2 Remove the rosemary sprig from the oil and discard. Remove the garlic from the oil, reserving both the garlic and oil. Add the garlic, anchovies if using, Parmesan cheese, salt, pepper, lemon rind and juice to a food processor and pulse until smooth.

3 In a medium bowl, gently fold the garlic mixture into the beans until they are well-coated. Let stand for a few minutes for the beans to absorb the flavours. Gently mix in the reserved olive oil, tomatoes and parsley.

CHICKEN AND COUSCOUS SALAD

Serves 4

300 ml (½ pint) chicken stock
200 g (7 oz) uncooked couscous
170 g (6 oz) diced cooked chicken
4 spring onions, green and white parts, thinly sliced
3 large radishes, diced
85 g (3 oz) cucumber, peeled, seeded and chopped
1 large ripe tomato, chopped
1 carrot, chopped
15 g (½ oz) fresh chopped flat leaf parsley
30 ml (2 tbsp) pine nuts, toasted
30 ml (2 tbsp) grated Parmesan cheese

For the dressing:

60 ml (4 tbsp) white wine vinegar
20 ml (1½ tbsp) extra virgin olive, rapeseed or pine nut oil
5 ml (1 tsp) ground cumin
2.5 ml (½ tsp) sea salt
Pinch freshly ground black pepper
1 clove garlic, chopped

1 Bring stock to the boil in a medium saucepan; gradually stir in couscous. Remove from the heat, cover and let stand for 5 minutes. Fluff with a fork.

2 Spoon the couscous into a large bowl and allow to cool slightly. Add the rest of the salad ingredients and toss gently to combine.

3 Prepare the dressing. Combine vinegar with the remaining ingredients and whisk. Drizzle the dressing over the salad and toss to combine.

Note: To toast nuts, heat a dry frying pan over a medium-high heat. Add the nuts, stirring frequently. As soon as they are fragrant, remove from the pan and cool.

ELEGANT TUNA SALAD

Serves 4-6

This is more like a French Salad Niçoise than a tuna salad. Use the best tinned tuna you can find.

30 ml (2 tbsp) home-made (page 116) or store-bought
    mayonnaise
30 ml (2 tbsp) capers, chopped
15 ml (1 tbsp) lemon juice
10 ml (2 tsp) fresh chopped tarragon
Sea salt and freshly ground black pepper to taste
2 x 200 g (14 oz) tinned yellowfin tuna in sunflower or olive
    oil, drained

For the salad dressing:

60 ml (4 tbsp) extra virgin olive oil
30 ml (2 tbsp) red wine vinegar or lemon juice
2.5 ml (½ tsp) Dijon mustard
Lettuce leaves
Baby plum tomatoes or cherry tomatoes
Kalamata or other ripe black olives
30 g (1 oz) flaked almonds

1 Make the dressing. In a mixing bowl combine the mayonnaise, capers, lemon juice, tarragon, salt and pepper.

2 Gently add the tuna, trying not to break it up too much.

3 Whisk together the olive oil, vinegar and mustard and season with sea salt and freshly ground black pepper to taste. Toss the lettuce and tomatoes in the dressing and place on a platter or individual salad plates.

4 Add the tuna mixture in the centre of the salad, arrange the olives around the tuna and top with the flaked almonds.

GREEN BEAN, RED ONION
AND PARMA HAM SALAD

Serves 4-6

600 g (1¼ lb) fresh green beans, topped and tailed
2 large red onions, thinly sliced
115 g (¼ lb) Parma ham, sliced into julienne strips
75 ml (5 tbsp) extra virgin olive oil
7.5 ml (1½ tsp) fresh lemon juice
5 ml (1 tsp) coarsely chopped fresh rosemary
4 ml (¾ tsp) sea salt
Pinch freshly ground black pepper
Good pinch red pepper flakes

1 In a large pan of boiling salted water, cook beans until crisp-tender, 2-3 minutes. Drain in colander, then immediately transfer to bowl of ice and water to stop cooking. Drain and pat dry. Refrigerate 1 hour or overnight.

2 One hour prior to serving, in a large bowl, combine beans, onions, Parma ham, olive oil, lemon juice, rosemary, salt, pepper and red pepper flakes. Toss gently and let stand at room temperature for 1 hour to blend flavours.

PANZANELLA (TUSCAN BREAD) SALAD

Serves 4

   340 g (12 oz) day-old Italian bread, torn into bite-size
      pieces
   40 ml (2½ tbsp) olive oil
   Sea salt and freshly ground black pepper to taste
   2 cloves garlic, finely chopped
   30 ml (2 tbsp) extra virgin olive oil
   15 ml (1 tbsp) balsamic vinegar
   2 medium-size ripe tomatoes, cut into wedges
   1 medium red salad onion, finely sliced
   10 fresh basil leaves, shredded
   8 large pitted and halved green olives
   55 g (2 oz) fresh mozzarella cheese, cut into bite-size
      pieces

1 Preheat the oven to 200°C (400°F/gas mark 6).

2 In a large bowl, toss the bread with 40 ml (2½ tbsp)
   olive oil, salt, pepper and garlic. Set the bowl aside.
   Place the bread on an ungreased baking sheet and
   toast in the oven until golden, about 5–10 minutes;
   allow to cool slightly.

3 In a small bowl, whisk together 30 ml (2 tbsp) olive oil
   and the balsamic vinegar. In the large bowl you used
   previously, gently toss together the bread, tomatoes,
   onion, basil, olives and mozzarella cheese. Toss with
   the vinaigrette and allow to stand for 20 minutes
   before serving.

MIXED GREENS WITH ASIAN DRESSING

Serves 4-6

   45 ml (3 tbsp) sesame seed oil
   30 ml (2 tbsp) soy sauce
   30 ml (2 tbsp) dark brown sugar
   15 ml (1 tbsp) rice wine vinegar or lime juice
   5 ml (1 tsp) freshly grated fresh ginger
   1-2 cloves garlic, finely chopped
   2 spring onions, green and white parts, finely chopped
   4-6 handfuls fresh salad greens

1 Whisk together the sesame seed oil, soy sauce, brown
   sugar, vinegar, ginger and garlic. Add the chopped
   spring onions and toss with the salad greens.

ROCKET, STRAWBERRY AND CHESHIRE CHEESE SALAD

Serves 4

   85 g (3 oz) fresh rocket leaves
   225 g (8 oz) strawberries, hulled
   140 g (5 oz) Cheshire cheese
   55 g (2 oz) chopped toasted hazelnuts

For the dressing:
   15 ml (1 tbsp) hazelnut oil
   45 ml (3 tbsp) extra virgin olive oil
   15-30 ml (1-2 tbsp) white balsamic vinegar
   2.5 ml (½ tsp) sugar
   Sea salt and freshly ground black pepper

1 Divide the rocket between four salad plates. If the
   strawberries are small, leave whole; if not, cut into
   halves or quarters and scatter them on top of the rocket.

2 Crumble the cheese on top of the strawberries.

3 Whisk the salad dressing ingredients together and
   drizzle on top of each salad, then top with the
   chopped hazelnuts.

HOME-MADE MAYONNAISE

Makes about 450 ml (¾ pint)

  2 free-range egg yolks
  2.5 ml (½ tsp) sea salt
  2.5 ml (½ tsp) powdered mustard
  Pinch sugar
  Pinch cayenne pepper
  20–25 ml (4–5 tsp) lemon juice
  360 ml (12 fl oz) mild olive or sunflower oil
  20 ml (4 tsp) hot water

1 Whisk the egg yolks, salt, mustard, sugar, cayenne
  pepper and 5 ml (1 tsp) of the lemon juice in a small
  bowl with an electric mixer at medium speed until
  very thick and a pale lemon colour.

2 Add about 60 ml (4 tbsp) oil, drop by drop, beating
  vigorously all the time. Whisk in another 5 ml (1 tsp)
  each of lemon juice and hot water, still beating
  vigorously. Repeat with a similar quantity of oil, lemon
  juice and water, beating the mixture constantly. Add
  120 ml (4 fl oz) oil in a slow, steady stream, still
  beating constantly, then mix in the remaining lemon
  juice and water. Slowly whisk in the remaining oil.

3 Spoon into a clean jar, cover and refrigerate until
  needed. Do not keep longer than one week.

Blender or food processor method: Place egg yolks,
mustard, sugar, cayenne pepper and 15 ml (1 tbsp) lemon
juice in the container of a blender or food processor and
process for 15 seconds. With the motor running, slowly
drizzle in 60 ml (4 tbsp) oil. As the mixture begins to
thicken, continue adding the oil in a slow, steady stream,
alternating with the hot water and lemon juice.
If necessary, stop and scrape the mixture down the
sides with a rubber spatula.

Note: This recipe contains raw eggs.

RASPBERRY WALNUT VINAIGRETTE

Makes about 240 ml (8 fl oz)

60 ml (4 tbsp) raspberry vinegar
180 ml (6 fl oz) walnut oil
15 ml (1 tbsp) Dijon mustard
5 ml (1 tsp) sea salt
5 ml (1 tsp) freshly ground black pepper
5 ml (1 tsp) sugar

Whisk the vinegar, oil and mustard together in a small
bowl. Stir in the salt, pepper and sugar then pour into a
screw-topped jar and refrigerate until needed.

WALNUT OIL DRESSING

Makes about 105 ml (3½ fl oz)

30 ml (2 tbsp) freshly squeezed lemon juice
75 ml (5 tbsp) walnut oil
Sea salt to taste

Whisk ingredients together in a small bowl, pour into a
screw-topped jar and refrigerate until needed.

CORDOBAN GAZPACHO

Serves 4

Similar to a traditional tomato gazpacho, but richer and smoother, this delightful cold soup is typical of Cordoba, Spain.

> 900 g (2 lb) ripe tomatoes, coarsely chopped
> 2 cloves garlic, chopped
> 60 ml (4 tbsp) sherry vinegar
> 240 ml (8 fl oz) extra virgin olive oil
> 5 ml (1 tsp) salt
> 12 whole blanched almonds
> 2 x day-old country-style bread rolls, about 85 g (3 oz)
>   each, torn into pieces and soaked in 240 ml (8 fl oz)
>   water for 10 minutes
> 1 egg yolk (optional)
> 2 hard-boiled eggs, peeled and finely chopped
> 85 g (3 oz) Spanish Iberico ham, finely chopped

1 In a large bowl, combine the tomatoes, garlic, vinegar, olive oil, salt, almonds and soaked bread plus any remaining water and mix well.

2 Working in batches if necessary, add the tomato mixture to a blender or food processor and process at high speed until smooth. For an especially smooth texture, pass the puréed mixture through a food mill. If using the egg, return the mixture to the blender or processor, add the egg yolk, and process until it is thoroughly incorporated.

3 Transfer to a bowl, cover, and refrigerate for at least 4 hours, or until well chilled.

4 Just before serving, taste the soup and adjust the seasoning if necessary. Ladle into chilled soup bowls, garnish with the chopped eggs and ham, and serve.

Note: This recipe contains an optional raw egg yolk.

ITALIAN ONION SOUP (ZUPPA DI CIPOLLE)

Serves 4-6

Similar to the famous French onion soup, the Italian version uses olive oil instead of butter, a light chicken or vegetable stock rather than beef stock, and Parmesan cheese instead of gruyère.

  45 ml (3 tbsp) extra virgin olive oil
  900 g (2 lb) mild white onions, thinly sliced
  Sea salt and freshly ground black pepper to taste
  120 ml (4 fl oz) dry white Italian wine, such as Pinot Grigio
      or Soave
  480 ml (16 fl oz) chicken or vegetable stock
  480 ml (16 fl oz) water
  4-6 thick slices crusty Italian bread, toasted
  Shaved Parmesan cheese

1 Heat the oil in a saucepan over a medium heat and add the onions, salt and pepper. Sauté until the onions begin to brown, about 10 minutes, then lower the heat and continue cooking until the onions are lightly browned, about 30 minutes.

2 Add the wine and cook until the liquid is reduced by half, about 5 minutes. Increase the heat to high, add the stock and water, and bring to the boil.

3 Reduce the heat and simmer, covered, for 30 minutes.

4 To serve, warm the soup bowls and place a slice of toasted bread in each bowl, ladle the soup over the bread, and use a cheese slicer to garnish with shavings of the Parmesan cheese.

SPANISH ALMOND SOUP (SOPA DE ALMENDRAS)

Serves 4-6

*Among the many contributions the Moors made to
Spanish cooking was the introduction of almonds.
This soup is a speciality of Grenada in southern Spain,
where the Arabic influence was strongest.*

>   45 ml (3 tbsp) olive oil
>   225 g (8 oz) blanched almonds
>   2-4 cloves garlic, coarsely chopped
>   3-4 slices white bread, cubed
>   12 black peppercorns
>   1.25 ml (¼ tsp) ground cumin
>   1.25 ml (¼ tsp) saffron strands
>   1.5 litres (2½ pints) chicken stock
>   5 ml (1 tsp) red wine vinegar
>   Chopped parsley for garnish

1 Heat the oil in a large pan over a medium heat and
  brown the almonds, garlic and bread until golden.

2 Remove the solids with a slotted spoon and combine
  with the peppercorns, cumin, and saffron in a blender
  or food processor. Process until smooth, adding a little
  chicken stock if necessary.

3 Combine the almond mixture, the remaining chicken
  stock and the vinegar in the pan and bring to the boil.
  Simmer, covered over a low heat for 15 minutes and
  serve garnished with chopped parsley.

MAIN
COURSES

ALPINE PORK ESCALOPES

Serves 4

>   8 thin pork escalopes
>   5 ml (1 tsp) paprika
>   10 ml (2 tsp) freshly ground black pepper
>   5 ml (1 tsp) dried rosemary
>   60 ml (4 tbsp) almond oil or macadamia nut oil
>   1 medium onion, sliced
>   225 g (8 oz) button mushrooms
>   15 ml (1 tbsp) flour
>   2.5 ml (½ tsp) sea salt
>   120 ml (4 fl oz) dry white wine
>   280 g (10 oz) gruyère cheese, thinly shaved
>   Small handful fresh parsley, chopped

1 Preheat the oven to 180°C (350°F/gas mark 4).

2 Season the pork with paprika, pepper and rosemary.
   In a frying pan, heat the oil and sear the pork on both
   sides. Remove the pork with a slotted spoon and place
   in one layer in a baking dish.

3 In the same frying pan over a medium heat, sauté the
   onion and mushrooms until golden. Remove from the
   pan with a slotted spoon and spread the mixture over
   the pork. Sprinkle with salt. Stir the flour into the oil
   remaining in the pan and cook for 1 minute. Add the
   wine and cook until the sauce thickens. Remove from
   the hob and pour over the pork. Sprinkle the pork with
   the shaved cheese and place in the preheated oven
   until the cheese melts.

4 Sprinkle with parsley. Serve with garlic mash and a
   green vegetable.

CRUMB-CRUSTED TILAPIA

Serves 4

> 450 g (1 lb) tilapia, cod, haddock or other white fish fillets,
>   skinned, about 2 cm (¾ in) thick
> About 55 g (2 oz) plain savoury biscuit crumbs
> 5 ml (1 tsp) grated lemon peel
> 1.25 ml (¼ tsp) sea salt
> Pinch freshly ground black pepper
> 60 ml (4 tbsp) milk
> 30 ml (2 tbsp) rapeseed or hemp seed oil
> 30 ml (2 tbsp) chopped pecan nuts

1 Move oven rack to a position slightly above centre of oven. Heat oven to 230°C (450°F/gas mark 8).

2 Cut the fish fillets into manageable pieces. In a shallow dish mix the biscuit crumbs, lemon peel, salt and pepper. Pour the milk into another shallow dish.

3 Dip the fish fillets into the milk, coat with the crumb mixture and place in an ungreased baking pan 33 x 23 cm (13 x 9 in). Drizzle the oil over the fish and sprinkle with the pecan nuts.

4 Bake, uncovered, for about 15-20 minutes or until the fish flakes easily with a fork.

CRISP NOODLE PANCAKE WITH STIR-FRIED VEGETABLES

Serves 4-6

For the sauce:

15 ml (1 tbsp) peanut (groundnut) oil
15 ml (1 tbsp) Chinese rice wine or dry sherry
15 ml (1 tbsp) soy sauce
15 ml (1 tbsp) honey
15 ml (1 tbsp) cornflour
5 ml (1 tsp) grated fresh ginger
1-2 cloves garlic, finely chopped
Hot red pepper flakes to taste (optional)

For the noodle pancake:

225 g (8 oz) Chinese noodles or thin spaghetti
5 ml (1 tsp) sesame seed oil
45 ml (3 tbsp) peanut (groundnut) oil

For the stir-fried vegetables:

45 ml (3 tbsp) peanut (groundnut) oil
5 ml (1 tsp) grated fresh ginger
2-4 cloves garlic, thinly sliced
3 spring onions, green and white parts, trimmed and cut
    into 2.5 cm (1 in) pieces
140 g (5 oz) mangetout, trimmed
115 g (4 oz) sliced mushrooms
225 g (8 oz) broccoli florets
1 red pepper, cored, seeded, and cut into julienne strips
1 green pepper, cored, seeded, and cut into julienne strips
100 g (3½ oz) tinned sliced water chestnuts

1 Mix the ingredients for the sauce in a small bowl and set aside.

2 Cook the noodles according to the package directions and drain. Rinse with cold water and drain again. Place the noodles on a clean kitchen towel and pat dry.

3 In another bowl, toss the noodles with the sesame oil.

4 Heat the peanut oil in a large frying pan over a
   medium heat and arrange the noodles in an even
   layer. Cook, covered, shaking the pan occasionally,
   until the noodles are browned and crisp on the
   bottom, about 5 minutes. Remove from the heat.
   Place a plate or board over the pan, invert both, and
   slide the noodles back into the pan, cooked-side up.
   Cook covered until the bottom is browned, about 3-4
   minutes. Remove from the heat.

5 Meanwhile, stir-fry the vegetables. Heat the peanut
   oil in another large frying pan or wok over a high
   heat. Sauté the ginger, garlic and spring onions for
   1 minute, then add the remaining vegetables. Sauté
   for 2 minutes and stir in the sauce. Continue cooking,
   stirring constantly, until the vegetables are crisp-
   tender and coated with the sauce, 2-3 minutes.

6 Transfer the cooked noodles to a serving platter, spoon
   the vegetables on top, and serve immediately.

GRILLED SALMON FILLET

Serves 6-8

900 g (2 lb) wild or farmed salmon fillet, skin on
30 ml (2 tbsp) olive oil
3 cloves garlic, crushed
Juice of one lemon
5 ml (1 tsp) Worcestershire sauce
60 ml (4 tbsp) light soy sauce
Lemon pepper seasoning

1 Preheat the grill. Set an oven rack 15 cm (6 in) from the heat.

2 Pat the salmon dry with a paper towel. Cut a piece of aluminium foil 10 cm (4 in) longer than the length of the salmon. Brush it with olive oil. Lay fillet, skin-side down on the foil. Fold edges of foil up around salmon to prevent juices from running out, leaving the top uncovered. Spread garlic evenly across salmon. Place on a baking sheet.

3 Combine lemon juice, Worcestershire sauce and soy sauce, and pour over fillet. Sprinkle liberally with seasoning.

4 Slide the salmon parcel into the oven. Cook 15-20 minutes, depending on thickness of fish. Do not turn. Salmon is done when the flesh has turned paler pink and flakes with a fork. Do not overcook.

5 Serve in portions with the cooking juices spooned on top. A green salad would be a good accompaniment.

PASTA WITH HAZELNUT PESTO

Serves 4

For the pesto:
115 g (4 oz) skinned hazelnuts, lightly toasted
55 g (2½ oz) fresh flat leaf parsley
2 large cloves garlic
120 ml (4 fl oz) extra virgin olive oil
60 ml (4 tbsp) hazelnut oil
Freshly-ground black pepper

600 g (1 lb) fusilli, penne or other pasta shapes
Parmesan cheese to serve

1 Tip all the ingredients for the pesto into a food
  processor or blender and pulse until smooth. Set aside.

2 Cook the pasta until al dente. Drain, reserving some of
  the cooking water. Keep hot.

3 Pour about half the pesto into a small jug, thinning it a
  bit with some of the pasta cooking water. Refrigerate
  the remainder in a screw-topped jar or airtight
  container for future use.

4 Serve the pasta tossed with the pesto. Top with
  Parmesan cheese.

Note: The pesto is also delicious served with roasted
vegetables or grilled fish.

HEALTHIER DUCK CONFIT

Serves 4

 4 duck leg portions with thighs attached, excess fat
    trimmed and reserved, about 900 g (2 lb)
 15 ml (1 tbsp) sea salt
 2.5 ml (½ tsp) freshly ground black pepper
 10 garlic cloves
 4 bay leaves
 4 sprigs fresh thyme
 7.5 ml (1½ tsp) black peppercorns
 Pinch sea salt
 1 litre (1¾ pints) grapeseed oil or enough to cover the duck
    legs
 Stir-fried vegetables or salad to serve

1 Place the duck legs skin-side down on a work surface.
  Sprinkle with the salt and pepper. Place the garlic, bay
  leaves and thyme on two of the duck legs and place
  the remaining two legs on top, skin-side up. Transfer
  the duck fat and legs to a plastic or glass container,
  cover and refrigerate for 1–2 days.

2 Preheat the oven to 110°C (225°F/gas mark ¼).

3 Take the duck from the refrigerator and remove the
  garlic, bay leaves, thyme and duck fat and reserve.
  Rinse the duck with cold water, rubbing off most of the
  salt and pepper. Pat dry with paper towels.

4 Put the reserved garlic, bay leaves, thyme and duck
  fat in the bottom of a heavy cast-iron baking dish.
  Sprinkle evenly with the peppercorns and salt. Place
  the duck legs on top, skin-side down. Add the
  grapeseed oil to cover the duck legs, cover and bake
  for 3–4 hours, until the meat is very tender and pulling
  away from the bone.

5 Remove from the oven and cool. Store, covered, in the
  refrigerator for up to one month.

6 To serve, remove the duck legs from the fat and crisp in a hot oven. Serve either with stir-fried vegetables or salad.

Note: The oil that the duck was cooked in may be used to roast potatoes, for stir-fries or to cook green beans.

SEARED MONKFISH WITH ROSEMARY, GARLIC AND HOT PEPPER

Serves 4

675 g (1½ lb) monkfish fillets cut diagonally into
    2.5 cm (1 in) slices
Sea salt and freshly ground black pepper
¼ cup macadamia nut oil
15 ml (1 tbsp) hot pepper flakes
30 ml (2 tbsp) chopped fresh rosemary
15 ml (1 tbsp) finely chopped garlic
240 ml (8 fl oz) dry white wine
240 ml (8 fl oz) fish stock
Handful chopped macadamia nuts (optional)

1 Sprinkle the fish fillets with salt and pepper. Heat the oil in a heavy sauté pan over amedium-high heat. Sear the monkfish slices quickly on both sides and set aside to keep warm.

2 Reduce the heat and add hot pepper flakes, rosemary, garlic, wine and stock. Cook over a high heat until the liquid is reduced by half, about 5 minutes. Season with salt and pepper. Reduce the heat and return the monkfish to the pan for a minute or two to finish cooking and coat with the sauce. Sprinkle with macadamia nuts, if using.

MOUSSAKA

Serves 6–8

30 ml (2 tbsp) olive oil
750 g (1½ lb) minced lamb or beef
1 medium onion, chopped
120 ml (4 fl oz) dry white wine
45 ml (3 tbsp) tomato purée
30 ml (2 tbsp) fresh chopped parsley
Sea salt and freshly ground black pepper to taste
1.5 kg (3 lb) aubergine
60–90 ml (4–6 tbsp) olive oil
1 recipe Béchamel Sauce (see p.131)
115 g (4 oz) fresh breadcrumbs
55 g (2 oz) grated Parmesan cheese
45 ml (3 tbsp) olive oil

1 Preheat the oven to 180°C (350°F/gas mark 4).

2 Heat the 30 ml (2 tbsp) olive oil in a large frying pan over a medium heat. Add the minced meat and onion and brown, stirring frequently to crumble the meat.

3 Add the wine, tomato purée, parsley, salt and pepper, and bring to the boil. Reduce the heat to low and simmer, covered, for 30 minutes, until most of the liquid has evaporated.

4 Meanwhile, cut the aubergine into slices 1 cm (½ in) thick and arrange on baking sheets. Brush both sides with olive oil and bake in the preheated oven for 25–30 minutes, until the aubergine is tender. Remove from the oven.

5 Arrange half the aubergine slices in the bottom of a medium baking dish. Sprinkle with half the breadcrumbs. Spread the meat mixture over the aubergine, followed by half the Parmesan cheese. Add another layer of aubergine, followed by the béchamel. Sprinkle the remaining Parmesan and breadcrumbs on top and drizzle with the 45 ml (3 tbsp) olive oil. Return to the oven and bake for 30–40 minutes, until the top is lightly browned.

BECHAMEL SAUCE

Makes 1 litre (1¾ pints)

85 g (3 oz) butter
45 g (1½ oz) flour
1 litre (1¾ pt) milk
Sea salt and white pepper to taste
Freshly-grated nutmeg

1 Melt the butter in a saucepan over a medium heat.

2 Stir in the flour and cook for 2 minutes, stirring all the time. Do not allow it to brown.

3 Whisk in the milk, making sure to dissolve any lumps that have formed.

4 Heat, stirring frequently, until the sauce comes to the boil and thickens. Season with salt, pepper and nutmeg.

POLENTA WITH MEDITERRANEAN
ROASTED VEGETABLES

Serves 4

For the polenta:

1 Prepare 250 g (9 oz) of instant polenta according to
packet instructions.

2 Stir in 100 g (3½ oz) grated Parmesan cheese and
55 g (2 oz) olive oil margarine.

3 Pour into a shallow square or rectangular dish, level
the top, cool, then refrigerate.

For the roast vegetables:
6 cloves garlic, whole with skin on
1 red onion, cut into 8 wedges
1 red pepper, cut into chunks
1 aubergine, cut into chunks
4 courgettes, sliced into rounds
2 sprigs fresh rosemary
60 ml (4 tbsp) extra virgin olive oil
15 ml (1 tbsp) sea salt

1 Preheat the oven to 200°C (400°F/gas mark 6).

2 Toss everything together and roast on a baking sheet
for about 30–40 minutes. Keep warm in the oven or on
a warmer.

Balsamic syrup:
240 ml (8 fl oz) balsamic vinegar
225 g (8 oz) soft brown sugar

Mix the vinegar and sugar together in a small pan over
medium heat and simmer until it is reduced by half and
looks slightly syrupy.

To finish:
    30 g (1 oz) toasted pine nuts
    200 g (7 oz) rocket leaves

To serve:

1 Cut polenta into 8 triangles.

2 Sauté in a frying pan with 30 ml (2 tbsp) olive oil until golden on both sides. Place two triangles on each plate. Pile roast vegetables on top, top with rocket and pine nuts and drizzle with the balsamic syrup.

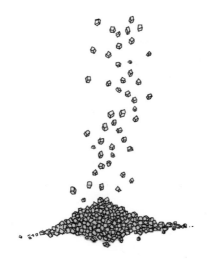

ITALIAN OVEN-FRIED CHICKEN

Serves 4

  55 g (2 oz) seasoned flour
  1 medium egg
  30 ml (2 tbsp) milk
  85 g (3 oz) fresh breadcrumbs
  45 g (1½ oz) freshly grated Parmesan cheese
  Sea salt and freshly ground black pepper
  1.5 kg (3 lb) chicken, cut into 8 pieces
  60 ml (4 tbsp) butter, sunflower or olive oil margarine
  60 ml (4 tbsp) mild olive oil
  Lemon wedges for garnish
  Parsley sprigs for garnish

1 Tip the seasoned flour onto a plate. Whisk the egg lightly with the milk in a shallow dish. Combine the breadcrumbs and Parmesan cheese in another shallow dish, generously seasoning with sea salt and freshly-ground black pepper.

2 Dust the chicken pieces lightly with the seasoned flour. Dip each piece into the egg-milk mixture, then roll in the breadcrumbs and Parmesan, patting the coating on firmly. Chill in the refrigerator for 1 hour.

3 Preheat the oven to 200°C (400°F/gas mark 6).

4 Melt the butter or margarine and oil in a roasting tin on the hob. When sizzling, arrange the chicken in one layer and spoon the fat over the pieces. Transfer the tin to the oven and bake, turning the chicken once or twice, for 40–45 minutes, until the chicken is tender and golden-brown.

5 Serve hot, garnished with lemon wedges and parsley sprigs.

AUBERGINE–COURGETTE LASAGNE

Serves 6–8

12 lasagne noodles, cooked
450 g (1 lb) ricotta cheese
225 g (8 oz) tomato sauce, without onions
450 g (1 lb) mozzarella cheese, shredded
1 medium aubergine, sliced 0.5 cm (¼ in) thin, lengthwise
3 green courgettes, sliced 0.5 cm (¼ in) thin, lengthwise
225 g (8 oz) spinach leaves
55 g (2 oz) grated Parmesan cheese
15 ml (1 tbsp) grapeseed oil
vegetables for top layer, either sliced mushrooms or big
    round tomato slices

1 Preheat the oven to 200°C (400°F/gas mark 6). Cover
   a large 23 x 30 cm (9 x 12 in) baking dish with a thin
   layer of grapeseed oil. Add 2 tablespoons of sauce,
   then lay out one layer of noodles to cover the bottom
   of the dish. Add enough aubergine and courgette to
   cover the noodles. Place spoonfuls of ricotta
   throughout the layers. Sprinkle some mozzarella and
   cover with some more sauce.

2 Place another layer of noodles, this time layering in
   the other direction. Repeat the process with the
   aubergine. Continue with spinach and repeat with
   remaining aubergine and courgette, alternating the
   vegetables and the direction of the noodles.

3 For top layer, create a nice pattern using either
   mushrooms or fresh tomato slices or mix both and
   cover with grated cheese.

4 Bake for 45 minutes. Remove from oven and let stand
   for about 15 minutes.

BAKED GOODS

CINNAMON STREUSEL COFFEECAKE

In America, where this sort of cake is very popular, 'coffeecake' refers to a cake served with coffee at a coffee morning perhaps, rather than a cake that is flavoured with coffee.

Makes one 25-cm (10-in) cake or two 900 g (2 lb) loaves*

Sunflower oil spray to grease pan
280 g (10 oz) caster sugar
75 ml (5 tbsp) rapeseed oil
2 large eggs
5 ml (1 tsp) vanilla extract
5 ml (1 tsp) almond extract
340 g (12 oz) plain flour
5 ml (1 tsp) baking powder
5 ml (1 tsp) bicarbonate of soda
2.5 ml (½ tsp) salt
400 g (14 oz) plain, vanilla or fruit-flavoured yogurt
Handful dried cranberries, cherries or cherry-berry mix
     (optional)
5 ml (1 tsp) plain flour (if using berries)

For the streusel:
40 g (1½ oz) marzipan, grated
40 g (1½ oz) flaked almonds
75 g (2½ oz) soft dark brown sugar
15 ml (1 tbsp) ground cinnamon

1 Preheat the oven to 180°C (350°F/gas mark 4). Spray a 25 cm (10 in) tube pan or 2 x 900 g (2 lb) loaf pans with cooking spray.

2 Make the streusel. In a small bowl, mix all the ingredients together and set aside.

3 In a large mixing bowl, mix the caster sugar and rapeseed oil together using an electric mixer. Whisk in the eggs, one at a time, beating well after each addition. Add the vanilla and almond extracts and mix well.

4 In another bowl combine the 340 g (12 oz) flour, baking powder and bicarbonate of soda. Stir well.

5 Add the flour mixture to the sugar mixture, alternating with the yogurt, beginning and ending with the flour and mixing after each addition.

6 Toss the berries, if using, with the 5ml (1 tsp) flour and fold into the batter.

7 Spoon approximately one-third of the batter into the prepared pan. Sprinkle with one-half the streusel mixture and repeat spooning the batter and the streusel. Spoon the remaining batter into the pan and level off.

8 Bake for 45 minutes in the centre of the oven, or until a wooden toothpick inserted into the centre of the cake comes out clean. Cool in the pan for 10 minutes on a wire rack, remove from the pan by shaking it gently and inverting the rack. Cool completely on the wire rack. When cool, store in an airtight tin.

* If you are baking loaves rather than a tube cake, baking time will be approximately 60 minutes. Use the toothpick test to check for doneness.

COURGETTE NUT MUFFINS

Makes 18 muffins

340 g (12 oz) plain flour
5 ml (1 tsp) baking powder
5 ml (1 tsp) bicarbonate of soda
5 ml (1 tsp) salt
5 ml (1 tsp) ground cinnamon
340 g (12 oz) Demerara sugar
4 large eggs
1 cup soybean or sunflower oil
225 g (8 oz) grated, unpeeled courgettes
2.5 ml (½ tsp) vanilla extract
115 g (4 oz) chopped walnuts or pecans
115 g (4 oz) sultanas

1 Preheat the oven to 180°C (350°F/gas mark 4). Lightly grease 18 muffin tins or line with paper liners.

2 In a bowl, sift the flour, baking powder, bicarbonate of soda, salt and cinnamon together. Set aside.

3 Combine sugar and eggs in a large mixing bowl and beat with an electric mixer at medium speed for 2 minutes.

4 Gradually add oil, beating constantly for 2-3 minutes. Add courgettes and vanilla extract and blend well. Stir in walnuts and sultanas. Fold in sifted dry ingredients just until batter is evenly moistened. Be careful not to overmix. Spoon the batter into the prepared muffin tins.

5 Bake for 25 minutes or until lightly browned and a wooden toothpick inserted into the centre comes out clean.

6 Remove from the oven and place the muffin tins on wire racks. Let stand 10 minutes, then turn muffins out onto wire racks to cool.

OUR DAILY BREAD

I haven't bought a loaf of bread since I bought a breadmaking machine more than five years ago. This is the loaf I bake every week, depending on the type of flour I have on hand. You can use white, wholemeal, granary or a combination. For the vegetable oil, corn, rapeseed and sunflower all give good results.

Makes one 750 g (1½ lb) loaf

> 300 ml (10 fl oz) tepid water (heated on medium in the microwave for 1 minute)
> 30 ml (2 tbsp) vegetable oil
> 5 ml (1 tsp) salt
> 7.5 ml (1½ tsp) sugar
> 30 ml (2 tbsp) dried milk powder
> 500 g (1 lb 2 oz) strong bread flour
> 1 sachet (10 ml/2 tsp) dried yeast

1 Put the ingredients into the breadmaker baking tin in the order specified for your particular model. Set the controls. If you have a choice, I have found that the basic white programme produces the nicest loaf, regardless of the flour used.

2 Once baked, it is best to remove the bread from the breadmaker as soon as possible. Shake the loaf from the tin and stand the right way up on a wire rack to cool. It will slice better if you leave it to cool first for at least 30 minutes.

SULTANA AND PINE NUT COOKIES

Makes 48 cookies

55 g (2 oz) sultanas
55 g (2 oz) dried apricots, chopped
115 g (4 oz) granulated sugar
75 ml (5 tbsp) mild light olive oil
2 egg whites
5 ml (1 tsp) grated lemon rind
5 ml (1 tsp) finely chopped fresh rosemary (optional)
225 g (8 oz) plain flour
4 ml (¾ tsp) baking powder
2.5 ml (½ tsp) bicarbonate of soda
55 g (2 oz) pine nuts

1 Combine sultanas and apricots with 15 ml (1 tbsp) water in a microwave-safe dish. Cover and heat on high for 1 minute. Let stand, covered, while preparing dough.

2 Mix the sugar, olive oil, egg whites, lemon rind and rosemary, if using, in a medium bowl, stirring vigorously until well-blended.

3 Mix the flour, baking powder and bicarbonate of soda in a small bowl. Add half the flour to the sugar mixture; stir until completely combined. Gradually add half of the remaining flour, stirring until combined. Stir or knead in remaining flour to make a stiff dough. Mix in sultanas and apricots (including any liquid) and pine nuts.

4 Shape dough into a cylinder about 5 cm x 30 cm (2 x 12 in). Wrap in cling film and freeze for several hours until firm, or up to one month.

5 To bake, preheat the oven to 190°C (375°F/gas mark 5). Using a sharp knife, cut frozen dough into 0.5 cm (¼ in) thick slices. Place on parchment-lined or ungreased baking sheets. Bake for 10-11 minutes until golden-brown on edges. Transfer cookies immediately onto wire racks to cool.

TREACLE COOKIES

Makes 24 cookies

    75 ml (5 tbsp) corn oil
    225 g (8 oz) caster sugar
    1 large egg
    60 ml (4 tbsp) treacle or molasses
    225 g (8 oz) plain flour
    10 ml (2 tsp) bicarbonate of soda
    5 ml (1 tsp) ground cinnamon
    5 ml (1 tsp) ground ginger
    2.5ml (½ tsp) ground cloves
    70 g (2½ oz) granulated sugar

1 Preheat the oven to 180°C (350°F/gas mark 4).

2 In a large bowl mix the corn oil and caster sugar.
   Add the egg and mix well. Stir in the treacle, flour,
   bicarbonate of soda, cinnamon, ginger and cloves.
   If necessary, add more flour to make a firm dough.

3 Shape the dough into 4 cm (1½ in) balls. Roll in the
   granulated sugar. Place 7.5 cm (3 in) apart on an
   ungreased baking sheet. Bake for 12–14 minutes, or
   until tops crack.

4 Remove from the oven and cool slightly. Gently lift the
   cookies onto wire racks to cool.

WALNUT BREAD

Makes one 750 g (1½ lb) loaf

  450 g (1 lb) strong brown or strong wholemeal flour
  6 ml (1¼ tsp) salt
  85 g (3 oz) chopped walnuts
  7.5 ml (1½ tsp) dried yeast*
  240 ml (8 fl oz) tepid water (heated on medium in the
      microwave for 1 minute)
  30 ml (2 tbsp) walnut oil
  30 ml (2 tbsp) mild-flavoured runny honey

1 Put the flour, salt, walnuts and yeast into a bowl.
  Mix to a soft dough with the oil, honey and water.

2 Turn the dough out onto a floured board and knead for
  10 minutes.

3 Shape into a small, round loaf and place onto a
  greased baking sheet. Leave to prove in a warm, draft-
  free place (an airing cupboard is ideal) until double in
  size.

4 Preheat the oven to 200°C (400°F/gas mark 6).

5 Bake for 30–35 minutes until lightly brown. When
  baked, the loaf should sound hollow when tapped on
  the bottom.

6 Remove from the oven and cool on a wire rack.

Note: You can also bake this bread in a breadmaking
machine. Put all the ingredients into the breadmaker tin
in the order listed by your manufacturer. Set to the basic
white programme for a 750 g (1½ lb) loaf.

*If you want the bread to prove faster, use 1 sachet
(10 ml/2 tsp) yeast.

DESSERTS

LEMON DESSERT CAKE

Makes one 18 cm (7 in) cake

170 g (6 oz) plain flour
Pinch salt
5 ml (1 tsp) baking powder
Grated rind of one lemon
140 g (5 oz) caster sugar
120 ml (4 fl oz) corn, groundnut or sunflower oil, plus oil
for greasing
90 ml (6 tbsp) water
2 medium eggs, separated
60 ml (4 tbsp) lemon curd

For the icing:
1 large egg white
170 g (6 oz) caster sugar
Pinch salt
Pinch cream of tartar
15 ml (1 tbsp) lemon juice

1 Preheat the oven to 180°C (350°F/gas mark 4).

2 Sift the flour, salt and baking powder into a bowl. Add
the lemon rind and sugar and mix with your fingers.
Make a well in the centre.

3 Whisk the oil, water and egg yolks together and pour
them into the well. Beat the mixture together with a
wooden spoon. It will be fairly stiff.

4 Whisk the egg whites until stiff peaks form and fold
into the cake mixture. Divide the batter between two
oiled 18 cm (7 in) sponge tins and bake for 20 minutes,
or until they are firm and have shrunk slightly from the
edges of the tins. Remove from the oven and place on
wire racks to cool.

5 When the cakes are cool, sandwich them together with
the lemon curd.

6 Make the icing. Combine the egg white, sugar, salt and cream of tartar in the top of a double boiler and using a wire whisk, whisk until the mixture is light and frothy.

7 Heat the water in the bottom pan and when it is simmering, place the top pan over and stir in the lemon juice, whisking the mixture constantly until it stands in stiff peaks, about 6–8 minutes.

8 Remove the pan from the heat and spread the icing over the top of the cake. Leave to set for 1 hour before serving.

GRILLED APRICOT SUNDAES WITH DARK CHOCOLATE AND PECANS

Serves 8

85 g (3 oz) roughly chopped pecans
8 fresh ripe apricots, cut in half and stoned
15 ml (1 tbsp) almond oil
115 g (4 oz) dark chocolate
1 litre (1¾ pints) good bought vanilla ice cream

1 Preheat the oven to 180°C (350°F/gas mark 4).

2 Place pecans on a rimmed baking sheet. Bake until lightly toasted, 3–5 minutes. Watch carefully because nuts burn easily. Remove from the oven and set aside.

3 Change the oven setting to grill on maximum heat or heat a hob-top grill pan. Brush the apricots with almond oil and put on the previously used baking sheet or grill pan. Grill the apricots on both sides until soft. Set aside.

4 Melt the chocolate in a suitable container in the microwave or on the hob.

5 To serve, place two apricot halves in each of eight dessert dishes. Top with a scoop of ice cream. Drizzle with melted chocolate and top with pecans.

RICOTTA, LEMON AND HONEY PIKELETS

Serves 4

250 g (9 oz) ricotta cheese
1 egg
45 ml (3 tbsp) plain flour
30 g (1 oz) caster sugar
Rind of one lemon, finely grated
30 ml (2 tbsp) sunflower or corn oil
60 ml (4 tbsp) honey, or to taste

1 Place the ricotta cheese, egg, flour, sugar and lemon rind in a medium bowl and, using a hand-held whisk or an electric mixer, beat until almost smooth. Cover and chill in the refrigerator for 30 minutes.

2 Heat the sunflower or corn oil in a frying pan over a medium heat and spoon tablespoonfuls of the mixture into the hot oil. Cook, turning, for 2-3 minutes or until golden on both sides. Transfer to a plate lined with paper towels and repeat with the remaining mixture.

3 Serve hot on dessert plates, drizzled with honey.

POACHED PEARS WITH RED WINE VINAIGRETTE

Serves 4

6 ripe dessert pears, peeled with stems intact
240 ml (8 fl oz) dry white wine
450 ml (¾ pint) water
30 ml (2 tbsp) granulated sugar
½ vanilla pod, halved lengthways
2 whole star anise
1 small cinnamon stick
Rind of one lemon, cut into strips
Rind of one orange, cut into strips
60 ml (4 tbsp) hazelnut oil
60 ml (4 tbsp) red wine vinegar

1 Trim the bottoms of the pears so they can stand upright and place in a large saucepan. Pour the wine and water into the pan and place over a high heat.

2 Sprinkle with the sugar, and add vanilla pod, star anise, cinnamon stick and lemon and orange rinds. Bring to the boil; reduce heat to medium-low, and simmer 20-25 minutes. Remove pan from the hob, and let cool completely. Reserve 60 ml (4 tbsp) poaching liquid. Transfer the pears to a bowl, cover, and chill in the refrigerator.

3 Place two of the poached pears in a blender or food processor and purée. Pour into a bowl. Whisk in the hazelnut oil, red wine vinegar and reserved poaching liquid. Cover, and refrigerate.

4 To serve, place pears in individual serving dishes and top with the prepared vinaigrette.

Recipes for Health and Beauty

This section of the book shows you how to make a wide range of both stimulating and soothing products for cleansing, toning and moisturising. Most of the recipes will not take more than 10 minutes to prepare and can be used immediately.

EQUIPMENT

All of your mixing and storing equipment must be scrupulously sterilised.

GLASS JARS AND BOTTLES

It is best to have a variety of shapes and sizes of jars and bottles available, and glass is definitely better than plastic as it can be sterilised at a high temperature after use, and can therefore be recycled. Amber glass jars and bottles are available from a number of sources on the internet and from some speciality craft shops.

GLASS MIXING BOWL AND GLASS ROD

A glass mixing bowl or jug and a glass rod are best for blending these products, as they can be properly sterilised after use. If you don't have a glass rod, a metal spoon can be used instead.

THE OILS

Essential oils should never be used neat; only with an appropriate light odourless carrier such as grapeseed oil, which is relatively inexpensive and easy to obtain. Grapeseed oil is also ideal as a base for massage blends or bath oils as it has a light, non-greasy texture and will not feel sticky. Almond oil is also a good all-purpose oil useful for massage blends.

Avocado oil is ideal for a drier, more mature skin and is also useful in anti-ageing blends.

CALENDULA OIL (*Calendula officinalis*)

Calendula oil is usually described as a macerated or infused oil, where the plant material is infused in oil. The botanical material is then removed leaving the oil with some of the properties of the botanical. Calendula oil has good anti-inflammatory properties, making it ideal for soothing wounds, rashes, eczema, nappy rash and other skin irritations. You can either make your own infusions by purchasing dried calendula petals or buy the oil already prepared.

As a massage oil, calendula has great healing, soothing and softening qualities which make it a good choice to include when mixing a massage oil or preparing a carrier oil blend. If you are looking for a base oil to use when suffering from skin problems, either with or without the addition of essential oils, then consider calendula oil.

JOJOBA OIL

Jojoba oil (pronounced *ho-ho-ba*) comes from a traditional healing plant. The golden oil is extracted from the seed pod and can be used in many ways. This oil is ideal in cosmetics as it has excellent lubricating qualities. Pure jojoba oil may be applied to all types of skin. Apply a few drops directly onto chapped or sore lips, dry skin or general skin disorders like eczema, psoriasis, dandruff or acne and, if applied lightly, it can act as a perfect facial moisturiser.

WATER

Water is a great breeding ground for bacteria. Even if you use distilled or filtered water for your recipes, it is safer to boil it before adding any other ingredients.

CAUTIONS

Pregnant women should check with a health practitioner before trying any of these recipes. Rosemary oil should not be used by those who have epilepsy. Do not use any citrus oil blends on your skin if you plan to expose yourself to the sun as this will make you more prone to sunburn. Always avoid contact with the eyes. Never store any of these blends in direct sunlight.

All the blends on these two pages may be used for massage or as intensive moisturisers either by adding a spoonful to your bath, or by applying to your skin after bathing. If you have extremely dry skin, enrich the blend by adding 5 ml (1 tsp) avocado oil.

MUSCLE SOOTHER

If you have a stiff neck or tense shoulders, this blend will help to ease muscle spasms. It is warming and soothing, reducing inflammation and relieving pain.

    1 drop chamomile oil
    2 drops rosemary oil
    2 drops lavender oil
    3 drops marjoram oil
    20 ml (4 tsp) grapeseed oil

Mix the essential oils together and blend with the grapeseed oil.

POOR CIRCULATION

If you have poor circulation, this blend will warm your hands and feet — whatever the weather. Rosemary oil can also be used to improve circulation; try using it in this blend instead of the vetiver.

    2 drops vetiver oil
    3 drops ginger oil
    3 drops grapefruit oil
    20 ml (4 tsp) grapeseed oil

Mix the essential oils together and blend with the grapeseed oil.

RELAXING SLEEP

This is excellent if you are having problems sleeping, either because of overwork, aching muscles or stress. Gently relaxing and comforting, it will have you sleepy in no time.

3 drops vetiver oil

4 drops lavender oil

4 drops orange oil

30 ml (2 tbsp) grapeseed oil

Mix the essential oils together and blend with the grapeseed oil.

BREATHE EASY

This is a wonderful oil which will help you breathe if you are suffering from a chest infection, hay fever or asthma. It will also help ease aches and pains associated with winter colds and flu.

3 drops cedarwood oil

3 drops frankincense oil

2 drops benzoin oil

20 ml (4 tsp) grapeseed oil

Mix the essential oils together and blend with the grapeseed oil.

CLEAR YOUR MIND

Clear your mind with this energising blend of oils, helping you to make decisions or motivate yourself. Lemongrass and ginger are both excellent for muscular aches and pains and together with geranium, will help alleviate digestive disorders.

3 drops ginger oil

2 drops lemongrass oil

3 drops geranium oil

20 ml (4 tsp) grapeseed oil

Mix the essential oils together and blend with the grapeseed oil.

JOJOBA MOISTURISING LOTION

Makes about 250 ml (about 8 fl oz)

100 ml (3½ fl oz) glycerine
75 ml (5 tbsp) rosewater
5 ml (1 tsp) avocado oil
5 ml (1 tsp) wheat germ oil
60 ml (4 tbsp) jojoba oil
8 drops lemon juice
few drops fragrance oil (optional)

1 Blend the ingredients together in a dish, using a wire whisk or electric mixer until they are completely emulsified.

2 Pour into a sterilised cosmetic bottle, seal tightly and store in the refrigerator.

3 Shake well before using.

HAIR STRENGTHENER

This is good for strengthening hair and giving it gloss.

Makes about 60 ml (4 tbsp)

30 ml (2 tbsp) almond oil
5 ml (1 tsp) chamomile oil
nettle leaves
birch leaves (can be bought as tea bags)
1 egg yolk, whisked
5 ml (1 tsp) runny honey
5 ml (1 tsp) lemon juice
2-3 drops rosemary oil

1 Heat the almond oil, then add the chamomile oil, nettle and birch leaves and set aside to infuse for 30 minutes.

2 Strain the mixture into a bowl and add the egg yolk, honey, lemon juice and rosemary oil. Whisk again.

3 To use, rub the mixture into damp hair and wrap up first with clingfilm and then a towel to keep the head warm.

4 Leave on for 10-20 minutes, and then wash hair as usual.

HOT OIL TREATMENT FOR HAIR

5 ml (1 tsp) soybean oil
10 ml (2 tsp) castor oil
few drops lavender or rosemary oil

1 Combine soybean oil and castor oil in a small saucepan and warm over a low heat.

2 Remove from the hob, add the lavender or rosemary oil and cool to a comfortable temperature.

3 Massage into wet hair and wrap head in a towel for 20 minutes.

4 Shampoo thoroughly and rinse.

ALMOND ROSEWATER BODY LOTION

Makes 165 ml (5½ fl oz)

60 ml (4 tbsp) rosewater
60 ml (4 tbsp) glycerine
30 ml (2 tbsp) witch hazel
15 ml (1 tbsp) almond oil

1 Mix together the rosewater and glycerine in a small bowl.

2 Add the witch hazel and almond oil and whisk to combine.

3 Pour into a suitable cosmetic bottle and store leftover mixture in the refrigerator.

COCOA MINT LIP BALM

Petroleum-based lip balms tend to dry out lips in the long run. This one is enriched with shea butter and cocoa butter and will leave your lips soft and luscious.

> 7.5 ml (1½ tsp) beeswax pellets
> 10 ml (2 tsp) shea butter
> 10 ml (2 tsp) cocoa butter
> 10 ml (2 tsp) almond oil
> 2.5 ml (½ tsp) vitamin E oil
> 10 drops peppermint oil (optional)

1 Place the beeswax, shea butter and cocoa butter in a heat-proof measuring beaker over a pan of boiling water.

2 When the mixture is completely melted, remove from the heat and stir with an ice-lolly stick or glass rod until blended.

3 Add the almond oil and vitamin E oil and stir to incorporate.

4 Add the peppermint oil if using and stir again. You may want to lessen the quantity of peppermint oil if you don't like the tingling effect it leaves on your lips, but it doesn't last very long.

5 While the mixture is still hot, pour into suitable cosmetic containers. Allow to cool, then seal.

6 If you should spill any of the mixture outside of the containers, leave to harden and wipe clean with a cloth.

LAVENDER CLEANSING LOTION

For all skin types

> 240 ml (8 fl oz) distilled water
> 1 chamomile tea bag
> 1 St John's wort tea bag*
> 90ml (6 tbsp) grapeseed oil
> 5ml (1 tsp) wheat germ oil
> 7.5 ml (1½ tsp) beeswax pellets
> 2.5 ml (½ tsp) bicarbonate of soda
> 8 drops lavender oil

1 Boil the distilled water and pour into a bowl. Drop in the chamomile and St John's wort teabags and leave to infuse until the water is cold.

2 Remove tea bags and discard. Set the infused water aside. Measure out 120 ml (4 fl oz) to use for this recipe. Discard the remainder.

3 Melt the beeswax with the grapeseed oil in a heatproof bowl over a small pan of water on a medium heat.

4 Meanwhile, dissolve sodium bicarbonate in the measured water in a pan over a low heat. Set aside.

5 When beeswax has melted, remove from the heat and cool slightly. Whisk in the infused water, drop by drop, until blended. Whisk in wheat germ oil and when cool, whisk in lavender oil. It should be a creamy coloured lotion.

6 Pour into a sterilised cosmetic container and store in the refrigerator.

7 To use, gently massage around eye area, neck and face, using upward strokes. Remove with a square of clean muslin, soaking the muslin first in hot water and patting on face to open pores, then soaking in cold water and patting on face to close pores.

*Can be purchased from health food shops

ROSE HAND CREAM

10 ml (2 tsp) beeswax pellets
30 ml (2 tbsp) lanolin
75 ml (5 tbsp) wheat germ oil
75 ml (5 tbsp) rosewater
3 drops rose oil

1 Place beeswax and lanolin in a sterilised heatproof container set over boiling water.

2 Stir with a glass stirring rod to melt and blend.

3 Slowly pour the wheat germ oil in a steady stream, stirring constantly.

4 Place a sugar thermometer in the mixture and heat to 80°C/160°F. Add the rosewater a little at a time, stirring until the mixture thickens. Let mixture cool to 50°C/105°F. Add the rose oil and stir thoroughly.

5 Remove from the water bath to cool, stirring thoroughly while cooling until the cream thickens and becomes smooth and white.

6 While still warm, fill sterilised cosmetic jar with spoonfuls of the mixture.

7 Store in a cool dark place.

TEMPTING TEA TREE MASSAGE OIL

20 ml (4 tsp) grapeseed oil
3 drops jasmine fragrance oil
2 drops tea tree oil
1 drop neroli fragrance oil

Blend ingredients well and warm gently before using.